FOOTSTEPS

Unforgettable Walks in Southeastern Virginia

Lou Belcher & Donna Fischl

FOOTSTEPS

Unforgettable
Walks in
Southeastern
Virginia

Lou Belcher & Donna Fischl

FOOTSTEPS
INCORPORATED

Chesapeake, Virginia

Footsteps: Unforgettable Walks in Southeastern Virginia
by Lou Belcher and Donna Fischl

Published by:
Footsteps, Inc.
P.O. Box 2302
Chesapeake, Va. 23327 USA

Library of Congress Cataloging - in Publication Data

Lou Belcher & Donna Fischl
Footsteps: Unforgettable Walks in Southeastern Virginia
Includes bibliographical references and index
ISBN 0-9657022-0-0: $12.95
1. Walking tours of southeastern Virginia
2. Regional history of specific locations.

Library of Congress Catalog Card Number: 97-90117

Cover art by :   Larry Moore
earthbase
orlando, florida

This book is dedicated to those who
preserve our history, protect our wildlife,
and manage our natural environments for
generations to come.

Table of Contents

Footsteps:

Introduction

The idea of *Footsteps: Unforgettable Walks in Southeastern Virginia* was conceived in a bookstore. As avid walkers, we naturally gravitate to books about the outdoors. One Saturday morning, while cruising the local bookstore, we found a book on favorite walks in England. We were so taken with it that we searched the regional section for something similar about our area (southeastern Virginia). The outcome of our search disappointed us. We found books that described hikes throughout the state, but not a single volume that rivaled that walking book on England.

We leafed through several hiking books hoping to find something to suit our purposes, but we found that they were geared more to the hard-core hikers -- the ones who spend a week or more on the Appalachian Trail, lugging 40 pound backpacks and dried food through the wilderness. Those books didn't meet our needs; we didn't want to travel halfway across the state for a three to a five-mile walk, and we had no intention of undertaking anything that involved sleeping in a tent or going to the bathroom in the woods. The idea of a walking book seemed simple enough to us. We just wanted something local and something that would give variety to our weekend walks.

Southeastern Virginia is steeped in history, from the Jamestown Settlement where the nation began to the Revolutionary War and Civil War battlefields and beyond; and rich in scenery, from the quaint architecture of Colonial Williamsburg to the Spanish moss draped on cypress trees in First Landing/Seashore State Park. Since the mild climate of southeastern Virginia lends itself to planning outdoor activities most of the year, we concluded that a book such

Footsteps: _____

as *Footsteps: Unforgettable Walks in Southeastern Virginia* would provide visitors as well as local walking enthusiasts a guide for planning an enjoyable way to see the many points of interest in this
area. Therefore, on that Saturday morning in the bookstore, we
committed ourselves to writing the book we envisioned, rather than
waiting for someone else to put it on the bookshelf for us.

We had no idea, at that point, the enormity of the project we had
undertaken. We soon found that we had to visit each of the areas
several times in order to ensure that the routes were easy to follow
and accurate. I'm sure that you, the reader, will appreciate this
attention to detail. Do not fear. You will not end up ten miles from
your car with no way back. In addition to accuracy, we felt we
should develop routes with all ages and abilities in mind -- not too
flat nor too hilly. Another criterion we established for the walks is
that for a walk to make it into the book, it had to be unforgettable.

The walks range in length from 1/8th mile to however far your
endurance and inventiveness will take you. At many of the sites, we
have provided the routes and mileage for possible walks. With this
information, you can devise a walk depending on the time you want
to spend, what you want to see in the area, and how far you want to
walk. In addition, we spent countless hours in the library research-
ing and extracting interesting facts about each area to enhance your
enjoyment of the walk.

There are basically four types of walks: city walks, nature walks,
historic walks, and beach walks. We have indicated in each section
if there are any fees to enter the area. For the walks that take place
at state parks, you can obtain an annual pass to enter all of them.
In most cases, the fees are low and should not deter you from visiting the area.

We've tried to lay out the book in a logical manner, so it'll be easy
for you to use. We've organized the walks by locality for easy refer-
ence. To enhance your walk at each location, we've provided background information, which includes a bit of the history of that particular location, and details regarding specific points of interest, so
that you can become your own tour guide. Where appropriate,
we've provided safety tips and have suggested a few precautions to

take to ensure an enjoyable walk. And, we've included that all-important information on the location of restrooms.

When undertaking the walks, remember that this is not a fitness program. Just put one foot in front of the other, set your own pace, and let your footsteps lead you through an unforgettable tour of southeastern Virginia.

Safety Tips:

1. wear comfortable walking shoes; clothing should be loose and layered; use sunscreen and sunwear when appropriate;

2. use insect spray, inspect self carefully after walks for tics, stay on marked paths; avoid touching or picking plants and flowers; do not approach wild animals;

3. listen to the local weather (or check with park staff for the day's conditions), bring water, walk with a partner, stop periodically to rest, and start back to the car before you get too tired.

Disclaimer: Risks are inherent in any outdoor activity. You must assume responsibility for your own actions and safety.

Chapter 1:
Chesapeake

Northwest River Park

Northwest River Park

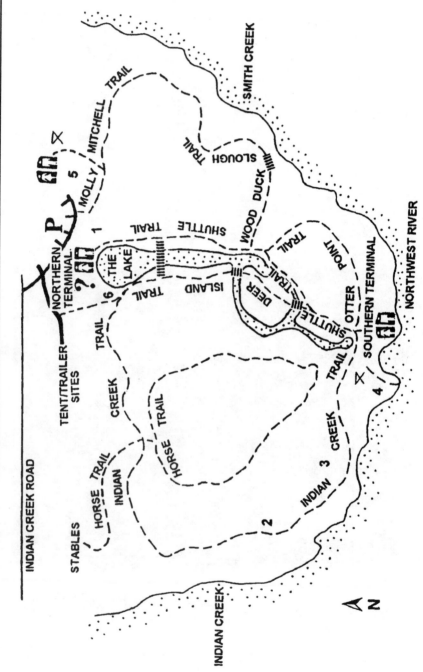

Key

? Ranger Station
P Parking
🚻 Restrooms
- - - Trails
║║║ Bridge
✕ Picnic Area
▬▬ Park Road

Walks

	Trail	Miles
1)	Fragrance Garden	Shuttle	1.25
2)	Fernpatch Meadow	Deer Island	0.75
3)	Moonshine Meadow	Indian Creek	2.5
4)	Marjie Ryan Memorial Walkway	Molly Mitchell	1.5
5)	Molly Mitchell Meadow	Wood Duck Slough	0.5
6)	Marian P. Whitehurst Memorial	Otter Point	1.0

Northwest River Park

Description

The nature trails at Northwest River Park offer walkers forested paths with an assortment of plants and trees, marsh areas, and sloughs (small branches of creeks that absorb the surplus water in the swamp when water levels become high) to explore. Throughout the park, water is visible almost wherever you walk. The 29 acre manmade lake (impoundment) was built in the center of the park and is used for boating and fishing. Indian Creek, Smith Creek, and the Northwest River border three sides of the park. All provide excellent opportunities for observing a variety of waterfowl. The trails are mainly flat, natural trails. The park is designed for a variety of outdoor activities. The walking trails are various lengths from .5 miles to 2.5 miles. You can combine trails and design a walk the length you desire in the environments you wish to experience.

Location

To reach Northwest River Park from I-64, take the Great Bridge-Battlefield Blvd. South (Rt. 168 South) exit. Follow Rt. 168 South for approximately 12 miles and turn left onto Indian Creek Road. Follow Indian Creek Road approximately 4 miles to the park entrance and turn right.

Parking and Facilities

Park in any of the four parking lots at the Northern Terminal. Restrooms are available at the Northern Terminal Ranger Station/ Camp Store, the Southern Terminal, and at the Molly Mitchell Meadow. Other activities available at the park include paddle boating, canoeing, camping, horse trails, picnic areas, a playground area, and fishing.

Background

Northwest River Park was built by the City of Chesapeake in 1975 and 1976. The 763 acres of land that make-up the park was purchased in three sections. The area nearest the Southern Terminal was used as a hunting and fishing camp before the purchase for the park. A second section, the Molly Mitchell Meadow in the day-use area, was purchased from and named for the woman who lived there. A third area purchased is the section surrounding the equestrian area.

Mrs. Marian Whitehurst, the former mayor of Chesapeake, formed a group called Friends of Chesapeake Parks that was instrumental in supporting the development of the park and in raising funds for it. She and the Chesapeake City Council dedicated the park in 1977. Northwest River Park was first called Indian Creek Park after the creek on the western side. Later, the name was changed to Northwest River Park after the river at its Southern Terminal. Today, the park is managed by the Chesapeake Parks and Recreation Department.

Northwest River Park has always been a community project. Enhancements, including two bridges built by boy scouts and the trail map at the entrance made by girl scouts, are examples of this. In addition, the park staff constructed the Marjie Ryan Memorial Walkway and hope to add more viewing areas in the near future.

Walks
The trail system in Northwest River Park lends itself to developing your own route, depending on the distance you want to walk.

1. *Shuttle Trail (1.25 miles):* This trail is named for the shuttle service from the Northern Terminal to the Southern Terminal that is provided on the hour on weekends between Memorial Day and Labor Day. This trail is a wide dirt-packed road and is closed to traffic except for the shuttle and park vehicles. Because it is an even surface, it is considered wheelchair accessible. The trail begins just to the left of the Northern Terminal and extends to the Southern Terminal. This is a beautiful wooded walk with a scenic view of the lake on your right.

2. *Deer Island Trail (.75 miles):* Take the road to the right of the Northern Terminal Ranger Station/Camp Store toward the

camping area and turn left onto Deer Island Trail. It follows along the other side of the lake. About halfway down, there is a bridge over a portion of the lake that provides a scenic view of the lake and water's edge. Deer Island Trail ends at the lower section of Shuttle Trail.

3. **Indian Creek Trail (2.5 miles):** Indian Creek Trail branches off from Deer Island Trail a short distance south of the Northern Terminal. It is named after Indian Creek which is the western border of the park. Indian Creek Trail follows the western side of the park down to the Southern Terminal. The bridge not far from the Southern Terminal end of this trail is called Eagle Bridge. It was built by Boy Scouts.

4. **Molly Mitchell Trail (1.5 mile):** Molly Mitchell Trail originates on the road between parking lot #3 and parking lot #4. The first portion of it is a flat path of packed gravel which is wheelchair accessible. There is a turnoff to the left a short distance down the trail where the packed gravel leads through Molly Mitchell Meadow to the parking lot area. The remainder of Molly Mitchell trail follows the eastern border of the park down to Wood Duck Trail. Molly Mitchell trail has a scenic slough approximately a third of the way along the trail, which is the natural habitat for wildlife, such as otters, squirrels, reptiles and wood ducks.

5. **Wood Duck Slough Trail (.5 mile):** Wood Duck Slough Trail starts at the bottom of Molly Mitchell Trail and ends at Shuttle Trail. It is named for the many wood ducks in the area. The bridge in the middle of this trail is called Blue Heron Bridge which was built by Boy Scouts.

6. **Otter Point Trail (1 mile):** Otter Point Trail starts and ends on Shuttle Trail. It skirts Smith Creek and Northwest River. Otter Point Trail was named for the point where Smith Creek meets Northwest River. If you're lucky, you may see otter in this area.

Points of Interest

1. *Fragrance Garden:* A boardwalk meanders 600 feet through the Fragrance Garden near the Ranger Station/Camp Store. Take a few extra minutes and enjoy this delight to the senses. It was built as a project of the Chesapeake Council of Garden Clubs.

2. *Fernpatch Meadow:* This meadow remains green throughout the year with its abundance of Christmas fern.

3. *Moonshine Meadow:* There have been over 30 moonshine sites discovered in Northwest River Park. Portions of four stills were found in Moonshine Meadow.

4. *Marjie Ryan Memorial Walkway:* This walkway was built in memory of the former city manager's wife. The walkway was built by park staff and leads through a wet marshy slough to a forested area and a bald cypress grove. It ends at a 15 foot platform, overlooking the river. The visibility from the viewing platform is one to one and a half miles. The walkway is handicapped accessible.

5. *Molly Mitchell Meadow:* This area has a playground and sheltered and unsheltered picnic areas complete with grills.

6. *Marian P. Whitehurst Memorial:* The memorial was built in honor of Marian Whitehurst who was the mayor of Chesapeake when the park land was purchased and the park was developed. It is fitting that the park contains this honor to her as she was instrumental in the early development of the park.

Chapter 2:
Colonial Triangle

Cornwallis' Cave, Yorktown

Colonial Williamsburg

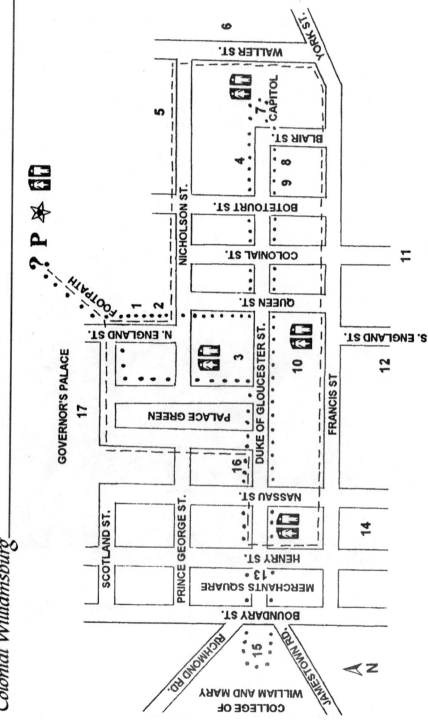

Key

?   Visitor Center

P   Parking

🚻   Restrooms

⭐   Start Here

••••   Walk 1 (3.2 miles)

‑ ‑ ‑ ‑   Walk 2 (3.0 miles)

1) Roberson's Windmill
2) Peyton Randolph House
3) Courthouse
4) Raleigh Tavern
5) Public Gaol
6) Christiana Campbell's Tavern
7) Capitol
8) King's Arms Tavern
9) Wetherburn Tavern

10) Magazine & Guardhouse
11) Williamsburg Inn
12) Williamsburg Lodge
13) Merchants Square
14) DeWitt Wallace Decorative Arts Gallery
15) Wren Building
16) Bruton Parish Church
17) Governor's Palace

Colonial Williamsburg

Description

A walk through Colonial Williamsburg is a walk back in time. The Colonial Williamsburg Foundation has meticulously recreated the feel of the beginning of our country. The authentic atmosphere is enhanced by horse drawn carriages, the fife and drum corps, and interpreters of Colonial Williamsburg dressed in period clothing. To choose one of the two walks offered here, scan through the Points of Interest for each walk and decide what sites interest you most. Walk 1 is 3.2 miles and takes you the length of Duke of Gloucester Street and to the Wren Building at William and Mary. Walk 2 is 3.0 miles and skirts the perimeter of the historic area with a good view of the gardens in the back yards of the restored buildings. Both walks start at the Visitor Center where you can buy a ticket for a look inside the buildings as you walk.

Location

The walks start at the Colonial Williamsburg Visitor Center. To reach the Visitor Center from I-64, take the Rt. 143 exit toward Colonial Williamsburg and follow the signs to Rt. 132 and to the Visitor Center.

Parking and Facilities

Parking and restrooms are available at the Visitor Center. In addition, restrooms are available throughout the historic area. You'll find a variety of shops in Merchants Square, and quaint eateries are available along Duke of Gloucester Street.

Background

When Jamestown was the seat of government, the area known as Williamsburg was called Middle Plantation. In 1633, some colonists from Jamestown settled at Middle Plantation to establish an outpost to protect the area against Indian attacks.

In 1698, the Fourth Statehouse at Jamestown burned to the ground, and the colonists finally gave up on Jamestown as the location of the capital after 90 years of struggle. Middle Plantation was chosen as the next location for the seat of colonial government. At that time, Middle Plantation consisted of a few houses, shops, a church, a couple of mills, and one building containing the College of William and Mary.

Middle Plantation had many advantages as the location for the capital. It was on high ground so they didn't have to deal with the swampland of Jamestown and the brackish water. It was inland, making it safe from naval bombardment; and it was relatively undeveloped, offering the opportunity to plan and build an appropriate capital. Great care was taken to plan out the new capital to intersperse shops of artisans, eating establishments and government buildings to make a well-centered city. Williamsburg became the capital in 1699 and was named for King William III of England.

Williamsburg remained the capital from 1699 until 1780. During that time, many of the men most prominent in the forming of the nation congregated in Williamsburg to share ideas and pass laws.

Francis Nicholson was governor when the capital moved from Jamestown to Williamsburg. He is credited with bringing economic stability to Virginia and strengthening the defenses, including fighting against pirates. Reverend James Blair, who was known as Commissary Blair, was the founder of William and Mary and served as its President. Blair was concerned about Nicholson's bizarre behaviors and went to England with charges against him of violent rages and illogical jealousies. As a consequence, Queen Anne recalled Nicholson.

Edmund Jennings served as the acting governor for four years after Nicholson was removed. Alexander Spotswood was the next governor and began his term of office in 1710. The Governor's Palace, Bruton Parish Church and the Powder Horn were built during his tenure, and life in Williamsburg picked up with councilmen, planters, and merchants filling Williamsburg with activity.

Under Spotswood, the Indian Act of 1714 was passed. It was designed to improve relations with the Indians and to make trade with them easier. An outpost was set up at Christiana for this purpose and to provide schooling for the Indian children. But, the act was repealed in 1717. The burgesses who opposed Spotswood closed Christiana after that.

One of Spotswood's special interests was stopping pirates off the coast of Virginia. He put together a group of men and went after the notorious Blackbeard. They caught and killed him off the coast of Ocracoke in North Carolina then sailed back with his head displayed on the front of the ship. That stopped Blackbeard, but other pirates continued.

Eventually, Spotswood, too, fell out of favor with Commissary Blair, and Blair had him removed. Hugh Drysdale followed Spotswood but only served four years. Robert "King" Carter followed him as acting governor for about a year before William Gooch took office in 1727. He served for 22 years. During his administration, the boundaries of the colonies were extended and Gooch worked to prevent slave revolts.

William Byrd II came into prominence during Gooch's administration. He was one of the most literate men of his time and served on the council for more than 30 years. His writings give readers a good view of life in those times. The first printing press in Virginia established the publication of the Virginia Gazette in Williamsburg during Gooch's tenure.

Robert Dinwiddie became the next governor in 1751. One of the events during his administration was the French and Indian War. Dinwiddie sent a 21 year old George Washington to demand that the French relinquish claim to land which they had seized. Washington went to Fort LeBoeuf to present Dinwiddie's demand to the French. The demand was rejected, but the trip was so full of hardship that Washington proved himself brave and able. At the age of 26, Washington was elected to the House of Burgesses.

After Dinwiddie ended his term in 1758, Francis Fauquier became governor. Young Thomas Jefferson, then a student at William and

Mary, dined with the governor several times and found him to be an able governor.

Patrick Henry also holds a prime spot in the history of Williamsburg. He, of course, became an eloquent orator. Even Thomas Jefferson, who was not a fan of Patrick Henry, praised his speech-making. The colonies were beginning to pull away from Great Britain at that time, and Patrick Henry contributed to this through his many speeches; one of the first was his speech in opposition to the Stamp Act.

Williamsburg was busy in pre-revolutionary activity. The taxes imposed by Great Britain, including the Stamp Act, the Townsend Act and later the taxation of tea that led to the Boston Tea Party, contributed to the rift between the colonists and Britain.

After Governor Fauquier died, Norborne Berkeley, Baron de Botetourt became governor. Botetourt is known for adjourning the House of Burgesses whenever they showed opposition to the edicts from England. When Botetourt adjourned the House of Burgesses because he was unsuccessful in getting them to accept the Townsend Act, the members of the House of Burgesses met without him at Raleigh Tavern to continue their opposition. Although the documents they devised were not legal, many colonists supported them anyway.

Botetourt died in 1770. He was followed in 1771 by John Murray, Earl of Dunmore. Shortly thereafter, the House of Burgesses established the Committee of Correspondence which was instrumental in building opposition to Britain. When the House of Burgesses denounced the closing of the port at Boston, Governor Dunmore adjourned the Assembly. Again, the leaders were not to be dismissed and they met at Raleigh Tavern. This time, they determined to unite with the other colonies and named a delegation to the first Continental Congress to be held in Philadelphia in September 1774. It was at this meeting that the Declaration of Rights was written.

Governor Dunmore was concerned over the Continental Congress and wanted to call the Virginia Assembly into session. The burgesses agreed to meet in Richmond but not in Williamsburg because they didn't want undo pressure from Dunmore. It was at this meeting that Patrick Henry offered a resolution that they develop their own militia separate from England. In response to his resolution, Governor Dunmore had British sailors remove the powder from the Powder Horn. However, when the new militia threatened to march on the Governor's Palace, he promised to return the powder.

In May 1775, Governor Dunmore fled to the British ship Fowey when he heard that there were threats on his life. He sailed to Norfolk, but he found he was not welcome there, either.

On May 6, 1776, the Virginia Convention met in Williamsburg. The convention wrote a constitution for the commonwealth, and a Declaration of Rights. These were taken to Philadelphia to the Continental Congress. The congress followed suit and appointed Thomas Jefferson and a committee to draft the Declaration of Independence. Patrick Henry was elected the first governor of the new Virginia after that, and he was so well-liked that he was re-elected twice.

Williamsburg served as the capital for 80 years. When they moved the capital to Richmond in 1780, Williamsburg became the county seat.

In the early twentieth century, Reverend W.A.R. Goodwin, who was the rector of Bruton Parish, provided the impetus for restoration of Williamsburg. He found a backer in John D. Rockefeller, Jr. Restoration was begun in 1926. They restored as many of the 18th century buildings as possible and replaced the 19th and 20th century buildings with the original 18th century buildings. Today, the Colonial Williamsburg Foundation manages Colonial Williamsburg.

Walks

1. ***Duke of Gloucester/William and Mary Walk (3.2 miles):*** Begin the walk at the flagpoles by the Visitor Center. Cross Rt. 132Y at the crosswalk and bear to the left onto the path leading to the colonial area. Follow the path to N. England Street. Walk along N. England Street and cross Nicholson Street and follow the path past the courthouse on Duke of Gloucester Street.

Turn left on Duke of Gloucester Street. Walk to Blair Street and turn right. Walk past the Capitol. Turn right and proceed along the opposite side of Duke of Gloucester Street. When you complete the length of Duke of Gloucester Street, cross Boundary Street to the campus of William and Mary. Bear left on the sidewalk past the Bafferton and the Office of the Provost. Turn right and walk behind the Wren Building. Turn right again on the other side of the Wren Building and walk back to Boundary Street. Cross Boundary Street and follow Duke of Gloucester Street to the Palace Green and turn left. Walk along the Palace Green to Governor's Palace. Turn right and return to N. England Street. Turn left onto N. England, then bear right onto the path leading back to the Visitor Center.

2. *Colonial Williamsburg Perimeter Walk (3.0 miles):* Begin the walk at the flagpoles by the Visitor Center. Cross Rt. 132Y at the crosswalk and bear to the left onto the path leading to the colonial area. Follow the path to N. England Street. Walk along N. England and turn left onto Nicholson Street. Follow Nicholson Street to Waller Street and turn right. Walk to Francis Street and turn right. Follow Francis Street to Henry Street and turn right. Walk one block to Duke of Gloucester Street and turn right. Continue on Duke of Gloucester Street to the Palace Green and turn left. Walk along the Palace Green to Governor's Palace. Turn right and return to N. England Street and turn left. Bear to the right onto the path leading back to the Visitor Center.

Points of Interest

1. *Robertson's Windmill:* William Robertson was the first owner of the windmill. He also served as the clerk of the council from 1698 until 1739. The windmill was important to the colonists because it was used to grind wheat which was the crop second only to tobacco. Robertson's Windmill is a post mill. It revolved on one large post and required close supervision by the miller, who rotated it to ensure that it faced the wind.

Footsteps:

2. **Peyton Randolph House:** Sir John Randolph was the only colonist knighted by the crown. He had two sons, Peyton and John. All the Randolphs served in colonial government. Peyton Randolph served as attorney general and was later elected speaker of the House of Burgesses (1766 - 1775). The American Revolution pulled the brothers to opposite sides. Peyton aligned himself with the side of the Americans, while John remained loyal to the crown. Peyton became president of the first Continental Congress in 1774. In 1775, John moved back to England. The house, named after Peyton Randolph, was home to one of the most prominent families of colonial times. It was built about 1715 and was the meeting place for gatherings important to the revolution.

3. **Courthouse:** An earlier courthouse stood at the corner of Francis and England. This one replaced it in 1770 and was used by Williamsburg and James City County until 1932. The courthouse served as the center of the community with legal notices posted in front. The proceedings at the courthouse were restricted to crimes not punishable by loss of life or limb. The General Court, housed in the Capitol, heard more serious cases. The Declaration of Independence was proclaimed to a large crowd at the courthouse.

4. **Raleigh Tavern:** Raleigh Tavern was established in 1717 and named after Sir Walter Raleigh, who was responsible for sending many of the colonists to Colonial Virginia. Raleigh Tavern served as a news and entertainment center as well as the place for social and political gatherings. The House of Burgesses met at Raleigh Tavern in 1769 when Governor Botetourt abruptly adjourned their session. Important patrons of the tavern included George Washington, Thomas Jefferson, Patrick Henry, Richard Henry and Francis Lightfoot Lee. In 1773, the Virginia Committee of Correspondence met at Raleigh Tavern. In December 1859, the tavern burned to the ground. Currently, behind the restored tavern is a bake shop.

5. **Public Gaol:** The Public Gaol was used until 1780. It is located just north of the Capitol. Accused criminals were imprisoned at the gaol until they were put on trial. It was built in

1704. In 1711, debtors cells were added. Then in 1722, quarters for the gaoler were added. At various times, it was used to house the mentally ill and as a military prison. In 1718, fifteen of Blackbeard's men were imprisoned in the public gaol.

6. **Christiana Campbell's Tavern:** The original building was used as a tavern starting in 1765. Mrs. Christiana Campbell became the proprietor in 1771. Before that, Mrs. Campbell ran another tavern from 1760 until 1769 at the site of the John Anderson House. George Washington often drank here with friends. They used a private room, so they could discuss issues of the day without being overheard.

7. **Capitol:** The Capitol building was built in the shape of an H with the House of Burgesses meeting on one side and the council meeting on the other. The House of Burgesses was made up of two members elected by the landowners for each county. The Council consisted of 12 councilmen appointed by the King for life. The Council and the House of Burgesses met separately, but if joint action was needed, they would meet in the second floor conference room that formed a passageway between the two buildings. The court at the Capitol heard both civil and criminal cases with stronger punishment than allowed at the courthouse. For example, death was the usual punishment for arson, forgery, burglary, piracy and stealing a horse. Many important political matters were discussed and settled at the Capitol. One of the most notable was the drafting of the Resolution of Independence on May 15, 1776 which led to the Declaration of Independence on July 4, 1776.

8. **King's Arms Tavern:** George Washington and William Byrd frequented King's Arms Tavern. The tavern was operated by Jane Vobe from 1772. She supplied food to the American troops during the American Revolution. After the revolution, the tavern was renamed Eagle Tavern.

9. **Wetherburn Tavern:** This tavern was named for Henry Wetherburn, who operated it from 1743 until he died in 1760. Wetherburn bought the property in 1738. Because one room measures 25 feet by 25 feet, it was often used for town meet-

ings, balls, parties, and political meetings. After Wetherburn died, a detailed list of the contents of his estate was made. This list plus an archeological excavation (1964 - 1966) resulted in an accurate restoration of the tavern. During the excavation, over 200,000 artifacts were recovered. The building was in continuous use for 200 years as a tavern, home, store, boarding home, and girl's school. After his wife died, Wetherburn married Mrs. Anne Marot Ingles Shields of Shield's Tavern.

10. *Magazine and Guardhouse:* In 1715, Governor Spotswood directed that the magazine be built to store weapons and ammunition. Later, due to the large amount of ammunition stored there, a wall was built around the magazine and the guardhouse was added. After the capital moved to Richmond, the magazine was used as a marketplace.

11. *Williamsburg Inn:* Many famous Americans and visiting dignitaries have stayed at the Williamsburg Inn. Harry S. Truman, Dwight D. Eisenhower, Richard M. Nixon, Gerald Ford, Ronald Reagan, Queen Elizabeth and Prince Phillip, and the Emperor and Empress of Japan stayed here. The Inn offers lodging to visitors of Colonial Williamsburg in the Inn and in reconstructed colonial houses in the historic district. In addition to the Inn, facilities include an 18 hole golf course, a 9 hole short course, tennis courts, and a swimming pool. The Williamsburg Inn was the site of the 1983 Economic Summit hosted by President Reagan.

12. *Williamsburg Lodge:* The Williamsburg Lodge and Conference Center provides lodging, a fitness center, and a conference center. It shares the golf and tennis facilities with the Williamsburg Inn. Adjacent to the lodge is the Craft House, which sells reproductions of Williamsburg antiques.

13. *Merchants Square:* Merchants Square is the shopping district of Colonial Williamsburg. It has restaurants, clothing stores, a book store, and souvenir shops. The stores are constructed to resemble 18th and 19th century stores. This was one of the first shopping centers to be built in America.

14. *DeWitt Wallace Decorative Arts Gallery:* The late DeWitt Wallace, founder of Reader's Digest, funded the museum. The gallery occupies 62,000 square feet of space. The contemporary museum offers exhibits of English and American decorative arts, masterworks, textiles, prints, ceramics as well as exhibits pertaining to Colonial Williamsburg.

15. *Wren Building at William and Mary:* The College of William and Mary was chartered in 1693. The Wren Building, the oldest academic building still in use, was the first structure restored by John D. Rockefeller, Jr. The architecture is said to have been influenced by Sir Christopher Wren. The cornerstone for the building was laid in 1695 and construction began that same year. The front and north wings were completed in 1700. Many famous men attended William and Mary, such as Thomas Jefferson, who enrolled at the age of 17. John Marshall and James Monroe are also famous alumni. Sir John Randolph, Peyton Randolph, John Randolph, Governor Botetourt, and Bishop James Madison are buried in the crypt below the Chapel. While the capital was under construction, the House of Burgesses met in the Great Hall of the Wren Building from 1700 to 1704. The statue in front of the building is of Governor Botetourt.

16. *Bruton Parish Church:* Bruton Parish was formed in 1674 by merging two earlier parishes. The first church on this site was built in 1683, but when the capital was moved to Williamsburg, a larger church structure was needed. They began construction of the present church building in 1711. It was completed in 1715 and has been in continuous use ever since. The church and government were closely tied during colonial times. The churchyard is the burial site of many important citizens and is surrounded by a brick wall.

17. *Governor's Palace:* During colonial times, most families lived in two to three room houses, so it was only natural that this residence became known as Governor's "Palace." The construction started in 1706, and Governor Alexander Spotswood supervised the building of it from 1710 until 1722. In 1716, he moved in while it was still under construction. Spotswood's goal of building a residence of distinction that would elevate the governorship was achieved. In 1753, the ballroom and supper room wing were added for entertaining. The Governor's Palace served the double purpose of residence and headquarters throughout the terms of seven royal governor's and the first two governors, Patrick Henry and Thomas Jefferson, of the new Commonwealth of Virginia. After the siege of Yorktown, the Governor's Palace was used as a hospital by Americans. They buried 156 soldiers in the graveyard on the grounds.

Jamestown Island Walk

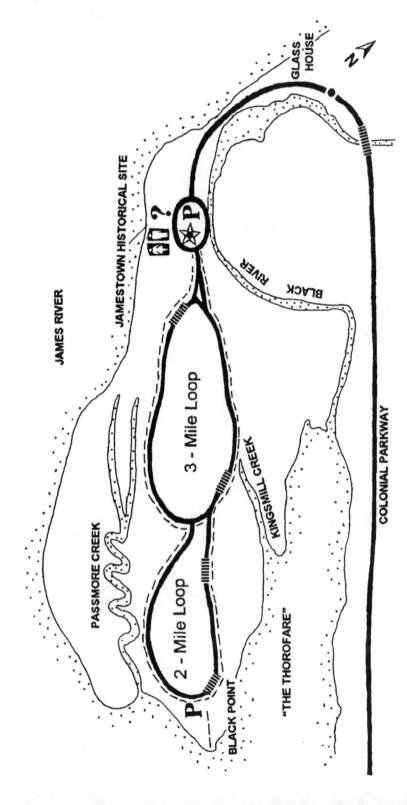

Key

- Park Entrance
- **P** Parking
- **?** Visitor Center
- 🚻 Restrooms
- ⭐ Start Here
- - - - Walk
- ||||| Bridge
- ▬▬ Park Road

Jamestown Site Walk

JAMES RIVER

ARCHEOLOGICAL EXCAVATIONS

CONFEDERATE FORT

P

TO PARK ENTRANCE

TO LOOP WALKS

Key

? Visitor Center

P Parking

🚹🚺 Restrooms

☆ Start Here

- - - Walk

||||||| Bridge

—— Park Road

1) Tercentenary Monument
2) Statue of Pocahontas
3) Old Church Tower
4) Statue of John Smith
5) Dale House
6) Memorial Cross

7) Third and Fourth Statehouses
8) Robert Hunt Shrine
9) New Towne Site
10) May-Hartwall House
11) Ambler House

Footsteps:
Jamestown Colonial National Historic Park

Description

Jamestown Colonial National Historic Park is the site of the first permanent settlement in North America. The park is surrounded by water including the James River, The Thorofare, and Back River. There are several possible walks at this park. One is a 3/4 mile walk through the site of historic Jamestown. Today, only the foundations of buildings and the Old Church Tower remain of Jamestown. This is a spot for history buffs. The Association for the Preservation of Virginia Antiquities and the National Park Service are working jointly on archeological excavations. This is where our country began, and it's a good opportunity to watch experts in the process of uncovering bits and pieces of that history. After leaving the historic site, you may want to walk one of the loop roads of Jamestown Island. The loops provide 2 mile, 3 mile and 5 mile routes in a setting virtually untouched from the time of the settlers. It takes little effort to imagine the lives of the settlers in this rustic environment.

After King James I issued a charter to the Virginia Company to establish the Virginia Colony, the Susan Constant, the Godspeed, and the Discovery set sail. The settlers arrived in Jamestown in May 1607. They chose Jamestown Island for their settlement because they thought the area would be easier to defend against Indians with only one border to protect. Unfortunately, they didn't take into account that the combination of marshland, woodlands, and brackish water did not make it particularly conducive to survival. The marshland, which makes this site a poor choice for producing crops, provides a picturesque site for walkers with tall reeds and wooded areas thick with birds and wildlife, and the scenic overlooks and bridges offer breathtaking views of the water.

Location

To reach Jamestown Colonial Historic National Park from I-64, take the Rt. 199 exit. Travel west on Rt. 199 toward Jamestown. Turn onto South Henry Street (N 132) and follow the signs to the Colonial Parkway. The Colonial Parkway will lead you to Jamestown. This is the same path the colonists would have taken from Williamsburg.

Parking and Facilities

There is a fee at the Contact Station at the entrance to the Jamestown Colonial National Historic Park. Follow the park road to the parking lot at the Visitor Center for the Jamestown Site Walk and for the 3 Mile Loop of the Jamestown Island Walk. For the 2 mile loop of the Jamestown Island Walk, there is a parking area at Black Point. Restrooms, interpretive programs, and a gift shop are available at the Visitor Center.

Background

Attempts to colonize North America began as early as 1588. After Roanoke Island in North Carolina failed, interest declined for a while during the Spanish War. But, Richard Hakluyt gathered supporters and petitioned King James I of England for permission to try again.

King James I eventually commissioned the Virginia Company to establish a settlement in North America. Three ships (the Susan Constant, the Godspeed, and the Discovery) set sail under Captain Christopher Newport on December 20, 1606. On April 26, 1607, they landed at Cape Henry. They explored several areas before choosing Jamestown and putting ashore on May 13, 1607.

Jamestown Colony had difficulties from the beginning. During the voyage, Edward Maria Wingfield and John Smith frequently quarreled, so John Smith was not pleased when they opened the sealed orders from the King that named Wingfield the first president of Jamestown Colony. In retaliation for their differences, Wingfield prevented Smith from taking his seat on the resident council.

The colonists used up most of their supplies during the voyage, consequently Captain Newport left for England in June 1607 to replenish the supplies and to bring back more colonists. While Newport was away, the colonists were not careful with the remaining rations of food and water. Disease and starvation resulted, and by the time Newport returned, only 38 of the original 104 settlers remained alive. To make matters worse, shortly after Newport returned in January 1608, fire destroyed all but three dwellings in Jamestown.

The settlers and those Newport had brought with him began to rebuild, but rations were low. Again, Newport left in April 1608 to return to England. He returned to Jamestown in October with more supplies and 70 more settlers.

Wingfield turned out to be a poor president. He was accused of hoarding supplies and was overthrown. John Ratcliffe was elected as the next president. He was not much better, but he did appoint John Smith as supply master. Through Smith's skill as a negotiator with the Indians, he was able to build supplies for Jamestown. It was during this period, however, that the Indians held Smith captive and Pocahontas saved him from execution by cradling his head in her lap when the Indians were about to beat him to death. After that, they set him free.

From the beginning of the colony, the Virginia Company searched for ways to profit from the colony. The first endeavor was glass-making which started in 1608. It was a natural choice of industry for the settlement because hardwoods were readily available. Due to the time-consuming struggle to survive, the industry failed. They tried glass-making once more in 1621. Again, it failed.

When Ratcliffe resigned at the end of his term, John Smith became the next president. Life in Jamestown improved under John Smith until July 1609 when Ratcliffe returned from England with a new charter and new orders. Dissension followed. Smith was severely wounded in a gunpowder explosion and was replaced by George Percy.

Under the new charter, 500 new settlers sailed for Jamestown in May 1609. The crossing was a difficult one. Many aboard ship suffered from the plague, and a hurricane wrecked the ship near Bermuda. Four hundred finally arrived in Jamestown in August 1609, but due to the shipwreck, they arrived without the supplies that the colony desperately needed. Famine followed.

Throughout its rocky beginning, the colonists continued to search for exportable crops. John Rolfe provided the answer. He is credited with starting the tobacco industry. The industry seemed such a boon that the colonists planted it everywhere, even in the streets.

John Rolfe is also known for marrying Pocahontas in 1613. After their marriage, the settlers lived more peacefully with the Indians as long as her father, Powhatan, was chief. But, when Opechanough became chief, things changed. He hated the English. On May 22, 1622, Opechanough attacked the colonists. One third of them lay dead and the killing lasted until the late 1620s.

In 1625 when King James I died, Charles I succeeded him. Under Charles I, Jamestown became a royal colony and Jamestown became Virginia's capital.

Sir Francis Wyatt was Virginia's first royal governor. Sir William Berkeley, who followed him, was governor for 35 years. Bacon's Rebellion is the most notable of the events during Berkeley's time in office. In 1676, civil war broke out when Nathaniel Bacon became the leader of those who were dissatisfied with Berkeley's unwillingness to protect them from the Indians.

Bacon wanted to lead his followers against the Indians, but Berkeley ordered him not to. Bacon disobeyed and later his defiance of this and subsequent orders from Berkeley came to be known as Bacon's Rebellion. When Bacon left to go after the Indians, Berkeley sent the militia after him. Bacon couldn't be found and Berkeley dismissed Bacon from the council.

Defying Berkeley, Bacon convinced the Occaneechees to attack the Susquehannock. Then Bacon fought the Occaneechees and killed them, too. Virginians celebrated him as a hero and his actions won him a seat in the House of Burgesses; however, Bacon was unsure whether to take his seat as Berkeley had ordered his arrest.

To ensure his safety, Bacon took 50 armed men with him when he went to Jamestown to attempt to claim his seat. Bacon anchored a sloop in the James River and sent a message to Berkeley asking to attend the House of Burgesses. In reply, Berkeley fired on the sloop, but Bacon retreated in time. Under the cover of night, Bacon snuck into town. He was caught and arrested, but Berkeley pardoned him when Bacon begged for forgiveness.

The next time Bacon showed up in Jamestown, the House of Burgesses was in the process of passing what came to be known as Bacon's Laws (more stringent measures in dealing with the Indians and one forbidding unlawful assembly). This time Bacon brought 500 men with him. Bacon again asked Berkeley to fight the Indians. When Berkeley denied his request, Bacon aimed his guns at the Statehouse. Consequently, the burgesses agreed to his demands and Bacon became General Bacon.

On June 26, 1676, Bacon left Jamestown after Indians. As soon as he departed, Berkeley proclaimed him a rebel. When he heard this, Bacon rallied as many men as he could find, intending to wrest the power from Berkeley.

Briefly, Berkeley retired to his country home at Green Spring, but Gloucester farmers ended his respite when they came to him complaining that Bacon had pressed them for their support and supplies, leaving them defenseless. Berkeley attempted to convince the men from Gloucester and Middlesex to ride against Bacon. They refused. Defeated, Berkeley retreated to the Eastern Shore. Meanwhile, Bacon gained strength, and he published a condemnation of Berkeley.

This infuriated Berkeley and renewed his determination to retake Jamestown. He gathered some supporters and sailed for Jamestown. When he arrived, he found 800 of Bacon's men occupying Jamestown. Berkeley offered them a pardon if they would give up; they accepted.

When Bacon heard of the activities in Jamestown, he was near Gloucester. He gathered as many men as he could find and returned to Jamestown. Bacon demoralized the men in Jamestown. He had captured their wives earlier, and he taunted the men of Jamestown by parading their wives in front of them. They soon gave in to Bacon and Berkeley fled. On September 19, 1676, Bacon entered Jamestown and burned it down. There's no telling what changes to government might have transpired if Bacon's Rebellion had continued, but we'll never know. In October of that same year, Bacon died of disease on the Eastern Shore, and the rebellion fell apart after that.

After the fire of 1676, the colonists rebuilt Jamestown once more. It was the seat of government for a while longer, but on October 31, 1698, Jamestown burned again. The seat of government was then moved to Williamsburg.

Over the following years, the property at Jamestown was consolidated into plantations. One of the most prominent of these was the Ambler Plantation.

In 1893, the Association for the Preservation of Virginia Antiquities (APVA) acquired 22.5 acres of the island. This included the site of the Brick Church built in 1639 and the last statehouse. They began archeological excavations in 1901. In 1934, all except the APVA section of Jamestown became part of the Colonial National Historic Park. Soon after acquiring Jamestown, archeologists from the National Park Service started excavation at Jamestown. Today, visitors can see the progress of current excavations.

In 1996, archeologists at Jamestown announced a major find. They uncovered part of the original Jamestown Fort, long thought to have eroded into the James River. They also found a body. Archeologists and historians are wondering if this might be the body of Captain George Kendall. This question stems from the discovery that the body has evidence of gunshots. There is a record that Kendall attempted to sail to Spain to tell Phillip II how bad things were in the Virginia colony. He was stopped by gunfire from the fort. There is no definitive evidence that this discovery is the body of Kendall, but the 1996 find at Jamestown shows us that there is still more to learn about our nation's history.

Jamestown Site Walk
Facing the James River from the Visitor Center, pass by the Tercentenary Monument (1). Turn right and pass the Statue of Pocahontas (2), the Old Church Tower (3), and the statue of John Smith (4). Continue straight to the Dale House (5) which houses the APVA

Footsteps:

archeological laboratory. Walk to the Memorial Cross (6) and just beyond it to the site of the Third and Fourth Statehouses (7). Turn right and walk to the pathway heading toward the river. Turn right and walk past the Robert Hunt Shrine (8). Continue to follow the path to the river. Turn left and walk along the river and pass the New Town Site (9). Continue along the river's edge then turn left and walk by the Hartwall House site (10). Turn left and pass by the Ambler House (11). Turn right and return to the Visitor Center.

Points of Interest

1. *Tercentenary Monument:* The first thing you see when stepping out of the Visitor Center is this 103 foot monument. It was constructed in 1907 in honor of the 300th anniversary of the founding of Jamestown.

2. *Statue of Pocahontas:* Pocahontas was one of the chief peacemakers of the early days of Jamestown. She saved John Smith from being beaten to death by the Powhatan Indians. In 1614, she married John Rolfe, which greatly improved relations for the settlers with the Indians. The settlers lived peacefully with the Powhatan Indians while Pocahontas' father, Chief Powhatan, was alive.

3. *Old Church Tower:* This is the only original structure still standing. Reverend Robert Hunt came to Jamestown with the first settlers. First, he established a simple church in the forest for worship. The settlers built a wooden church inside the fort after that. In January 1608, it burned. Another frame church was built within the fort. Again, in 1617, another frame church (this time outside the fort walls where the Memorial Church stands today) replaced it. In 1639, it was torn down and the brick church was built on the same site. The tower was built some time after 1647 as an addition to the brick church. In 1907, the National Society of Colonial Dames of America gave the Memorial Church to the Association for the Preservation of Virginia Antiquities as a gift.

4. *Statue of John Smith:* John Smith was president of the Virginia Council in 1608 - 1609. His skills as a negotiator with the Indians helped the settlers maintain supplies in the early years.

5. *Dale House:* This building is the home of the Association for the Preservation of Virginia Antiquities Archeological Laboratory for Jamestown. Many of the items uncovered at Jamestown are on display here.

6. *Memorial Cross:* Many lost their lives during the winter of 1609 - 1610. Their graves are marked by the Memorial Cross.

7. *Third and Fourth Statehouses:* The foundations of the Third and Fourth Statehouses are evident here. The Fourth Statehouse was the last built for Jamestown. When it burned in 1698, the capital was moved to Williamsburg.

8. *Robert Hunt Shrine:* Robert Hunt was the colony's first Anglican minister. He arrived in Jamestown with the first settlers.

9. *New Towne Site:* This area was developed after 1620.

10. *May-Hartwall House:* This house was built around 1661. Henry Hartwall and his family lived here. He was the founder of William and Mary College as well as an author and clerk of the General Assembly.

11. *Ambler House:* This house was built in 1750. It was of Georgian style and was the house for one of the largest plantations after the capital moved to Williamsburg and the land was consolidated into plantations.

Jamestown Island Walks

1. *3 Mile Loop:* Begin at the parking lot at the Visitor Center and bear to the left on the first loop of the island drive so that you'll be walking against traffic. Follow the loop. Once you cross the bridge, bear to the right to continue the other side of the loop back to the parking lot.

2. *2 Mile Loop:* Park at the parking area at Black Point. Follow the loop to the left to ensure that you are walking against traffic. Turn right at the crossover to continue the loop back to the parking area.

Footsteps: _____

3. *5 Mile Walk:* Park at either the Visitor Center or Black Point. Walk against traffic for safety. Do not cross over at the end of the 2 or 3 mile loop. Walk the outside perimeter of the loop roads and back to where you parked.

Old Country Road

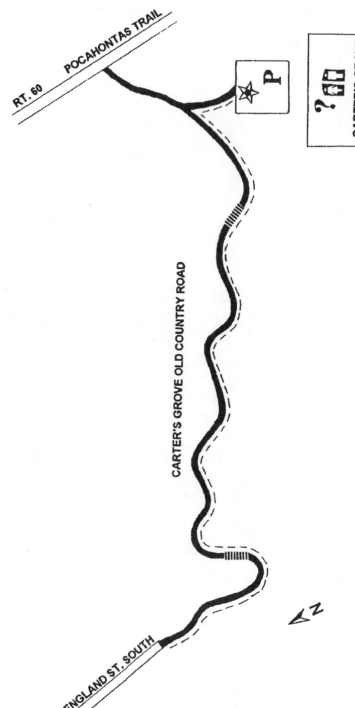

Key

?   Information

P   Parking

🚻   Restrooms

⭐   Start Here

- - -   Walk

||||| Bridge

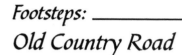
Old Country Road

Description

If you're looking for a longer walk in a setting reminiscent of colonial times, Carter's Grove Old Country Road is the perfect location. The road extends eight miles and connects Carter's Grove Plantation to Colonial Williamsburg. During colonial times, the Country Road was used by the inhabitants of Carter's Grove Plantation to reach Williamsburg. It is representative of the roads that connected plantations with nearby towns and is an example of the preservation of the history of the entire area. The walk offers visitors an opportunity to step back in time and to enjoy the countryside our ancestors enjoyed.

Mile markers along the road tell you how far you've gone, so you can keep track of the distance you walk. The Old Country Road walk starts at the Reception Center of Carter's Grove Plantation. The single lane portion of it traverses beautiful woodlands, marsh areas, and open fields for 6 1/4 miles of picturesque scenery. Deer and many other woodland animals call this home. Waterfowl can be seen searching for food in the marsh. After 6 1/4 miles, the road widens as it enters Colonial Williamsburg. Those interested in touring a colonial plantation can combine the walk with a visit to Carter's Grove Plantation.

Location

The walk begins at the Carter's Grove Plantation Reception Center parking lot which is located 8 miles southeast of Colonial Williamsburg. To reach the parking area, take Rt. 60 east from Colonial Williamsburg. Watch for signs on Rt. 60 directing you to Carter's Grove Plantation. Turn right off Rt. 60 onto the Country Road. Then turn left into the parking area.

Parking and Facilities

Parking, refreshments, and restrooms are available at the Carter's Grove Reception Center. The Reception Center has a gift shop and an outdoor patio area with tables where you can enjoy a soft drink or snack. If you have a pass to Colonial Williamsburg, a visit to Carter's Grove is usually included. Otherwise, there is a fee to tour the plantation.

Safety Tip

The Country Road is one-way going from Carter's Grove Plantation to Williamsburg. It is a one lane dirt road for the first 6 1/4 miles then widens to a paved two lane road. Traffic is light on the road, but it's a good idea to watch for vehicles and step to the side of the road when one passes.

Background

Carter's Grove Plantation, at one end of the Country Road, sits on the banks of the James River. The first settlers of this area, however, arrived nearly 150 years before the plantation was built. The Martin's Hundred Society of London sent 220 settlers to this portion of the James River to build a fort. They named the area Wolstenholme Towne after Sir John Wolstenholme.

Wolstenholme Towne didn't survive long. In the attack of May 22, 1622 by the Powhatan Indians, 58 settlers died and 20 were captured. Attempts to rebuild were unsuccessful. The settlement disappeared before 1700.

In 1690, Robert "King" Carter gave his daughter, Elizabeth, the land of Carter's Grove Plantation as a wedding present when she married Nathaniel Burwell. With the gift, he stipulated that the area always be called Carter's Grove. Carter's Grove has always been a working plantation. It's major crops include meat and dairy products, corn, wheat, and apples.

Elizabeth Burwell and her husband built one wing of the plantation house the year they were married and the opposite wing five to ten years later. The main house wasn't built until 1750.

Footsteps:

When Nathaniel Burwell died in 1721, their son, Carter Burwell, inherited the plantation. He is responsible for building the main house. It was finished in 1755 and is an excellent example of Georgian architecture. One of the rooms within the house has come to be known as the Refusal Room because it is said that George Washington asked Mary Cary to marry him in that room, and she refused. Also, Thomas Jefferson asked Rebecca Burwell to marry him in that room, and she refused.

Carter Burwell died in 1756, six months after the house was completed. The plantation stayed in the Burwell family until 1838 when Phillip Lewis Carter Burwell sold it to Thomas Wynne. Between 1838 and 1900, the plantation changed hands 9 times. In 1928, Mr. and Mrs. Archibald McCrea bought the plantation and restored it. They are responsible for raising the roof and adding the third floor. Carter's Grove is currently owned by the Colonial Williamsburg Foundation and it has remained much the same as it was when Mrs. McCrea died in 1960.

Walk

Begin the walk at the parking lot of the Carter's Grove Plantation Reception Center. Turn left from the parking lot onto the Old Country Road and walk as far as you want. Use the mile markers on the road to judge the distance you want to walk before turning around to return to the parking area.

Points of Interest in the Vicinity

1. **Carters Grove Plantation:** On the banks of the James River, Carter's Grove Plantation sits on a beautiful piece of land befitting a plantation. Although Robert "King" Carter gave his daughter this land in 1690, it wasn't until 1755 that the main house was completed by King Carter's grandson, Carter Burwell. The house remained in the Burwell family until 1838. Visiting the plantation, it's easy to imagine life in colonial times. The grounds are beautifully maintained by the Colonial Williamsburg Foundation.

2. **Wolstenholme Towne:** The first residents of the property where Carter's Grove Plantation sits today, arrived just after the establishment of Jamestown Colony, farther up river. The Martin's

Hundred Society of London sent English colonists to establish a settlement in the early 17th century. Two hundred and twenty settlers built a fort at Wolstenholme Towne in 1618. Archeologists have uncovered the fort, statehouses, dwellings and farms of Wolstenholme Towne on Carter's Grove property. In 1991, the Winthrop Rockefeller Archeology Museum was established southeast of the plantation house to display the relics discovered at Wolstenholme.

Waller Mill Park

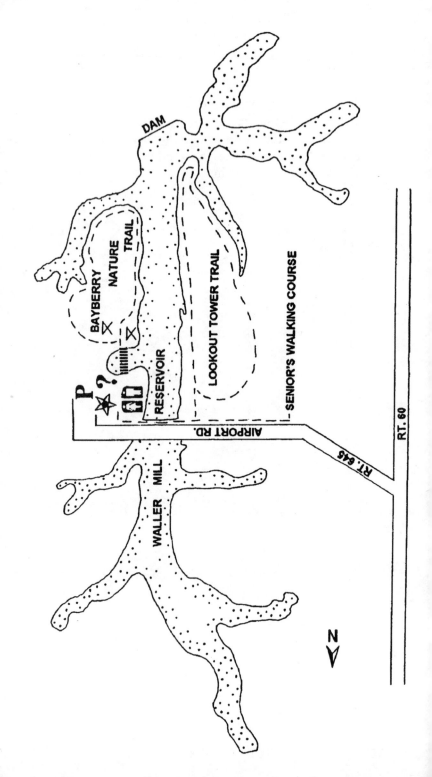

DAM

BAYBERRY NATURE TRAIL

P

RESERVOIR

LOOKOUT TOWER TRAIL

SENIOR'S WALKING COURSE

AIRPORT RD.

WALLER MILL

RT. 645

RT. 60

N

Walks

Trail	Miles
Bayberry Nature	1.5
Lookout Tower	2.65

Key

? Information

P Parking

🚻 Restrooms

⭐ Start Here

– – – Trail

✕ Picnic Area

▌▌▌ Bridge

Waller Mill Park

Description

Waller Mill Park offers two scenic nature trails for walkers. Both are cut through the wooded hillsides overlooking the quiet beauty of Waller Mill Reservoir. The shorter trail, Bayberry Nature Trail, is 1.5 miles long. The Bayberry Nature Trail was designed to be used as an educational experience for those who wish to learn about the vegetation and wildlife of the area. There are 75 markers that correspond to the guidebook for an interpretive self-guided tour of the trail. The terrain is easy to moderately difficult with a couple of inclines that ascend to overlooks. The other trail, Lookout Tower Trail, is a 2.65 mile loop on the opposite side of the lake. The terrain is similar, but this trail has an observation tower where you can catch a panoramic view of the reservoir.

Location

From Williamsburg, take Rt. 60 west to Rt. 645 (Airport Road). Turn right onto Rt. 645 then watch for the sign into the park and turn right into the parking area.

From I-64, take the Rt. 143 exit towards Williamsburg. Bear to the right onto Rt. 132. Turn right onto Rt. 60 Bypass. Follow Rt. 60 East to 645 (Airport Road). Turn right onto Rt. 645 then watch for the sign to the park. Turn right into the parking area.

Parking and Facilities

Parking, picnic areas, and restrooms are available near the Ranger Station. There are sheltered (rental) and unsheltered picnic areas, and grills available. Boats, canoes and paddle boats are available for rental at the Ranger Station for a closer look at the lush environment of the reservoir.

Background

The city of Williamsburg built Waller Mill Park and opened it in 1972. They developed the park on 2,350 acres of land surrounding the Waller Mill Reservoir. The 343 acre reservoir provides a beautiful walking environment on two nature trails. The Bayberry Nature Trail is 1.5 miles long and winds through semi-hilly terrain for a woodland walk with picturesque views of the reservoir. The Lookout Tower Trail is 2.65 miles in length with terrain similar to that found on the Bayberry Nature Trail. Lookout Tower Trail has an observation tower for a spectacular view of the upper and lower sections of the reservoir. Both trails have scenic overlooks and benches to relax and enjoy the scenery. The city designed the park to showcase the reservoir. There are beautiful views of it from both of the trails.

There are activities for outdoor enthusiasts with a variety of interests at Waller Mill Park. In addition to the walking trails, mountain bikers will enjoy the challenging 4.1 mile bike trail, and there is a 1.0 mile senior walking course with 14 stretching exercise stations to add diversity to the walk. For jogging enthusiasts, there is a Fitness Trail with 12 exercise stations. The diversity of activities at this park makes Waller Mill Park a spot with something for all ages.

Walks

1. *Bayberry Nature Trail (1.5 miles):* The walk begins in the picnic area across the bridge from the Ranger Station. Bear to the right after you cross the bridge and follow the trail markers.

2. *Lookout Tower Trail (2.65 miles):* The walk begins across the parking lot from the Ranger Station. After you cross over the boat tunnel that connects the lower and upper portions of the reservoir, turn left onto the trail and follow the trail markers.

Points of Interest

1. *Dogwood Bike Trail (4.1 miles):* The Dogwood Trail was designed for mountain bikers. It is 4.1 miles in length and provides an interesting route through challenging terrain.

Footsteps: _____

2. *Fitness Trail:* This trail is for joggers. It is one mile in length over hilly terrain interspersed with 12 exercise stations.

3. *Senior Walking Course (1 mile):* The Senior Walking Course is designed with 14 stretching exercise stations.

York River State Park

York River State Park

N

RT. 607
RT. 606 LANDING RD.
CROAKER
P

TASKINAS CREEK

Taskinas

YORK RIVER STATE PARK RD.
RT. 696
RT. 606

P?

Woodstock Pond

Beaver

Mattaponi

Laurel Glen

Pamunkey
Majestic Oak
Backbone
Spurr

Powhatan Forks

YORK RIVER

Key

- • Contact Station
- ❓ Ranger Station
- 🚻🍴 Restrooms
- - - - Trails
- ||||||| Bridge
- ✕ Picnic Area
- ▬ Park Road

Walks

Trail	Miles
Taskinas	1.6
Woodstock Pond	1.3
Beaver	0.6
Mattaponi	1.4
Backbone	1.3
Laurel Glen	0.4
Pamunkey	0.8
Spurr	0.2
Majestic Oak	1.0
Powhatan Forks	1.4

Footsteps:
York River State Park

Description

The York River paints a scenic backdrop for a nature walk at York River State Park. The trails follow carefully planned routes to optimize the gentle transition from forest to marshland. There are at least 15 miles of hiking, biking, and horse trails within the park. The walking trails range from .2 miles to 1.6 miles in length and can be combined for longer walks. This park is of special interest to nature lovers. You're apt to see a variety of species of birds within the park as well as deer, beaver and raccoons. Wood ducks and heron gravitate to the Wood Duck Pond area, and owls, hawks and warblers are often sighted, too. Fiddler crabs congregate at low tide on mud flats and sand flats when their burrows are exposed. Visitors find their antics fun to watch. There is much to learn from York River State Park. Besides being an excellent spot for bird and wildlife watching, the park is a Chesapeake Bay National Estuarine Research Reserve. Ongoing research continues to provide an understanding and interpretation of the estuary system, so researchers are better able to preserve it. Also, an archeological site was excavated within the park. It is on the National Register of Historic Places.

Location

From Interstate 64, take Route 607. When you reach Croaker, turn right onto Rt. 606 (Riverview Road). Then turn left onto Rt. 696 (York River Park Road) to the Visitor Center. To reach Croaker Landing, take Route 607 and turn right onto Rt. 605 (Croaker Landing Road).

Parking and Facilities

Parking and restrooms are available at the Visitor Center at the end of York River Park Road and at Croaker Landing. There is a parking fee. Other park activities include self-guided and guided canoe trips, paddle boats and Jon boats, playgrounds, picnic areas, horse trails, a mountain bike trail, horseshoe pits, volleyball courts, concession stands, gift shop, boat ramp and fitness trail.

Background

Tobacco was the main product of the colonists in the 17th century and the early 18th century. The colonists stored some of their tobacco in a public tobacco warehouse on this land before it was shipped to England. The 2,505 acre park was established in 1980 to preserve the natural environment of the area and this piece of the early history of the country. At low tide the remains of the wooden road used during the tobacco warehouse period are visible along the Taskinas Creek.

Long before the colonists, the ocean covered this area to Richmond. Fossils remain today as evidence of that time and many visitors successfully search the banks of the river and streams for remains of earlier times. You might find evidence of whales, porpoise and fish as well as prehistoric shells. Also, before the colonists, early inhabitants of the area were Algonquin speaking tribes. Chief Powhatan ruled over tribes along the York River. He had as many as 30 tribes including 8,000 to 9,000 Indians.

An important feature of the park and evidence of the dedication of the Department of Conservation and Recreation to preserving the delicate balance of the environment is the maintenance of the Taskinas Creek and the marsh surrounding it as a Chesapeake Bay National Estuarine Research Reserve. Because saltwater meets freshwater here, this area serves as a nursery for marine life of the Chesapeake Bay. During spring through fall, the park offers a two hour guided canoe trip to interpret this environment for visitors.

Walks

1. *Taskinas Creek Trail (1.6 miles):* The Taskinas Creek Trail starts to the right side of the parking lot when facing the parking lot from the Visitor Center. An interpretive booklet describes numbered markers on this trail. During the first portion of the trail, you'll walk past the picnic shelter area to a loop through the Taskinas Creek and marsh area.

Footsteps:

2. **Woodstock Pond Trail (1.3 miles):** The Woodstock Pond Trail starts on the York River side of the Visitor Center and is a 1.3 mile loop. There are several trails that intersect for a variety of walks.

   a) **Beaver Trail (.6 miles):** Partway around the Woodstock Pond, you can pick up Beaver Trail (.6) miles which keeps you close to the pond when Woodstock Pond Trail heads toward Backbone Trail.

   b) **Mattaponi Trail (1.4 miles):** This trail is an extension along the York River of the Woodstock Pond Trail. When Woodstock Pond Trail turns back away from the York River, you can continue your walk along the river on the Mattaponi Trail. This trail follows a level ridge top for a while then descends to a tidal marsh.

3. **Backbone Trail (1.3 miles):** From the Woodstock Pond Trail, Backbone Trail heads southeast through the park and connects to another series of walking trails, known as the Back Country Trails. With all of these trails, watch your distance. You will have to walk back to where you parked your car from any of these.

   a) **Laurel Glen Trail (.4 miles):** From Backbone Trail, turn left onto Laurel Glen Trail. This is a short walk to a loop at the end. It highlights the mountain laurel pine and oak woodlands. At the far end is an overlook to a wetland area.

   b) **Pamunkey Trail (.8 miles):** Turn left off Backbone Trail onto Pamunkey Trail. On this trail, you'll travel through an oak and maple woods. The trail heads straight toward the York River. It descends to an observation tower which is a great place for photography.

   c) **Spurr Trail (.2 miles):** Spurr Trail is a short trail that joins the Pamunkey Trail to the Majestic Oak Trail.

d) *Majestic Oak Trail (1 mile):* Majestic Oak Trail is the next left off Backbone Trail. You can also reach it from the Pamunkey Trail by taking Spurr Trail (.2 miles) which cuts across from Pamunkey to Majestic Oak. If you take Spurr Trail, turn left onto Majestic Oak Trail. It goes straight toward the York River. It intersects the north fork of the Powhatan Trail at that end, and you can either return by the same route or turn right and enjoy the Powhatan Trail boardwalk.

e) *Powhatan Forks Trail (1.4 miles):* At the beginning of Majestic Oak Trail where it intersects to the left with Spurr Trail, turn right onto the Powhatan Forks Trail. Halfway up the trail, you can turn right and walk the trail approximately .3 miles or you can go straight to the North Fork of the Powhatan Trail and enjoy the boardwalk through a tidal marsh.

Points of Interest:

1. *Croaker Landing:* An archeological site was excavated from January through March of 1978 at Croaker Landing, then it was put on the National Register of Historic Places. Vessels and ceramic wares dating back to between 1000 B.C. to 1 A.D. and between 1 A.D. to 900 A.D. were found at the site. You can visit Croaker Landing by taking Rt. 607 then turning right onto Rt. 605 (Croaker Landing Road). The boat ramp is also on Croaker Landing Road. Parking and restrooms are available.

2. *Chesapeake Bay National Estuarine Research Reserve:* The Taskinas Creek and the surrounding marsh make up the Chesapeake Bay National Estuarine Research Reserve. This is a nursery for marine life of the Chesapeake Bay. It is carefully preserved by the park to maintain the delicate balance of the ecosystems of the bay. More information about this important work can be obtained at the Visitor Center. Each year, a day in September is set aside as Estuaries Day to point out how important this work is.

3. **Woodstock Pond:** This pond was first stocked with large mouth bass and bluegills in the late 1950s. Today it is stocked with golden shiners, eels, sunfish, and catfish. Beaver also live here, and you can see evidence of their work where they have left chewed tree stumps around the pond. Other inhabitants of the area are the many birds, including osprey, great blue heron, and wood ducks. In addition there are deer and racoons in this area.

Yorktown Battlefields

Key

? Visitor Center

P Parking

🚻 Restrooms

- - - - Walks/Historical Tour Road

✕ Picnic Area

▓ Bridge

D Redoubts 9 & 10
E Moore House
F Surrender Field
H Washington's Headquarters
K French Encampment Loop
L Untouched British Redoubt

Walks

Trail	Miles
D – E	1.5
E – F	1.75
F – H	2.0
H – K	3.25
H – L	3.25

Description

The peaceful fields and streams of the Yorktown Battlefields weren't always so serene. During the Revolutionary War Siege of 1781 and again during the Civil War, cannon balls flew and artillery fire filled the air with the sounds and sights of war. There are unlimited walking possibilities at the battlefields. The location provides a walking environment that combines the beauty of a nature walk with the history of the beginning of our country. The National Park Service has devised a 7 mile auto Battlefield Tour and a 9 mile auto Encampment Tour. By parking at strategically placed parking areas, you can also walk portions of these routes for a closer look at the historic battlefields as well as the beautifully preserved natural environments. With planning, you can walk routes from 1.5 miles to 7 or more miles. Be sure to stop at the Visitor Center where information is available. Enjoy the view from the observation deck on the second floor of the Visitor Center to gain a panoramic view of the battlefields.

Location

To reach Yorktown from the south, use I-64 and take the J. Clyde Morris Blvd. North (Rt. 17) exit. Follow Rt. 17 to Yorktown. When you get close to Yorktown, you'll see signs for Yorktown Battlefield. Follow the signs to the Visitor Center. From the north, use I-64 and take the Yorktown exit onto the Colonial Parkway. Follow the Colonial Parkway to Yorktown and follow the signs to the Visitor Center.

Parking and Facilities

Parking and restrooms are available at the Visitor Center. For the walks, parking is available at areas designated as D, E, F, and H.

Safety Tip

Because the auto-tour roads are also used by slow-moving cars touring the area, it is important to watch for traffic.

Background

Yorktown was already an important port town and well known for the many historical figures who lived there, but the Siege of 1781 on the Yorktown battlefields sealed the area's place in history. The major players in the battles of the Revolutionary War at Yorktown were the American forces under General George Washington and their French allies versus the British troops under Lord Earl Cornwallis.

Prior to the Siege of 1781 at Yorktown and before Washington and his troops arrived, the American forces in Virginia consisted of 2,000 militia and 1,000 light infantry commanded by Lafayette. Lafayette knew that he couldn't overtake the British forces on his own. So, he decided to attempt to keep the British forces from uniting while he waited for reinforcements.

Because the British blocked Petersburg, Virginia, Lafayette decided to attempt to lead them out of their position. So, he headed across Virginia toward Yorktown. As predicted, Cornwallis followed, but Lafayette successfully eluded him and united with Anthony Wayne and his 10,000 men who had marched down from Pennsylvania. Joining forces with Wayne gave Lafayette the strength he needed to drive Cornwallis back to Williamsburg without engaging him in battle.

Cornwallis, also, was reluctant to engage in battle without reinforcements. He waited in Williamsburg while he sent word to Sir Henry Clinton in New York for reinforcements. Because Washington was breathing down his neck in New York, Clinton denied Cornwallis' request and ordered him to send reinforcements to New York.

Cornwallis left Williamsburg and headed toward Portsmouth to transport the troops to New York. Before the troops were sent, however, Clinton changed his mind and ordered Cornwallis to fortify Old Point Comfort (Fort Monroe today) in order to establish a port to accommodate larger British ships. Cornwallis decided to fortify Yorktown and Gloucester Point instead of Old Point Comfort. By August 22, 1781, Cornwallis and his 7,000 men had made their way to Yorktown.

Meanwhile, Lafayette held a position near Williamsburg because he still felt his troops weren't strong enough to win an engagement with Cornwallis. He patiently waited for Washington.

While Clinton prepared his troops for battle against Washington in New York, Washington slipped away and moved his troops toward Virginia. At about the same time, De Grasse sailed 28 ships toward the Chesapeake Bay. With 3,300 French troops under the command of Marquis de Saint-Simon, the ships arrived at the end of August. On September 5th, British ships under the command of Admiral Graves arrived in the area. The ships engaged in battle, and the British ships withdrew out of firing range. Eventually, Admiral Graves decided he had no chance of winning, so he withdrew the British ships completely and moved them to New York.

Washington marched from the Hudson Valley to Virginia and joined up with Lafayette at Williamsburg. In preparation on September 28, 1781, Washington and Lafayette marched toward Yorktown. On September 29, 1781, Cornwallis moved the British troops from their field positions to positions closer to town.

When Washington and Lafayette arrived in the Yorktown area, they moved into the abandoned British positions and sent some men to Gloucester to prevent a British escape in that direction. Washington and Lafayette bombarded the British repeatedly as they maneuvered their troops closer and closer to Redoubts 9 and 10. When Washington and Layfayette stormed Redoubts 9 and 10, Cornwallis made plans for escape; but, by the advance planning of placing some of their men in Gloucester, Washington and Lafayette successfully thwarted the British escape attempt.

Although Clinton had promised to join Cornwallis, he didn't arrive, and Cornwallis, with his men sick and beaten, gave up on receiving assistance. He wrote to Washington on October 17th and proposed a meeting at Moore House to draw up the terms of surrender. On October 18th, 1781, Lieutenant Colonel Thomas Dundas and Major Alexander Ross for the British met with Viscounte de Noailles and Lieutenant Colonel John Laurens at Moore House to establish the procedures for surrender. When the time came for surrender on October 19, 1781, Cornwallis feigned illness so that he wouldn't have to personally surrender. He sent Brigadier Charles O'Hara to make the surrender. Although the war didn't officially end for another two years, this was the last and definitive battle of the Revolutionary War.

During the years between the Siege of 1781 and the Civil War, the damage to Yorktown was repaired and the town of Yorktown reverted to a quiet town. The Civil War broke that quiet during 1862.

General George B. McClellan was assigned by Lincoln to take the Confederate capital at Richmond, Virginia. He started his Peninsula Campaign at Fort Monroe. McClellan's first point of engagement was at Yorktown against the Confederates under the command of Major General John B. Magruder.

When the Union troops arrived at Yorktown, the Confederates sent frequent artillery fire their way. The Union troops responded by testing the Confederate defense line occasionally. Placement of troops during the Siege of 1862 mirrored that of 1781. The skirmishes lasted for about a month, but the Confederates eventually retreated when they determined that they couldn't win if the Union troops decided to do more than test their defense line.

Although there was no clear outcome at Yorktown, by delaying McClellan and the Union troops for a month, Magruder gave other Confederate troops time to reach Richmond and add to the defense of the capital.

Today much of Yorktown and the battlefields are maintained by the National Park Service, U.S. Department of the Interior. President Herbert Hoover established the area as the Colonial National Monument in 1930. The Yorktown portion of it consisted of 2,500 acres at that time. In 1931, acreage was added to the Yorktown portion to bring the total to 4,500 acres.

Footsteps:

Walks

The areas at Yorktown are marked with letters by the National Park Service. We have used these same letter markings for the possible walks to avoid confusion. Devise a walk to suit the distance you want to go.

1. **D - E (3 miles round trip):** Redoubts 9 and 10 are at D. From D to E (Moore House) is 1.5 miles one way. You can park at either end. Starting at D, you will pass the site of the first Siege Line and the site of the Deposit where siege materials were stored. When you reach Wormley Creek Crossing, turn left and walk to Moore House.

2. **E - F (3.5 miles round trip):** The walk from Moore House to Surrender Field is 1.75 miles one way. On this walk you'll pass the site of the headquarters of Major Benjamin Lincoln who was second in command of the American army, the site where the Virginia Militia under the command of Thomas Nelson, Jr. was quartered, the site of Layfayette's headquarters, and the site of the American Field Hospital. When you reach Highway 704, be cautious as you cross the road and walk a short distance up Surrender Road to the left turn into Surrender Field. You can park at either E or F.

3. **F - H (4 miles round trip):** The walk from Surrender Field to the site of Washington's Headquarters is 2 miles one way. Along this walk, you'll pass the site of the American Artillery Park, the site of the French Hospital, and the site of the Headquarters of Henry Knox. You can park at either F or H.

4. **H - K or L (6.5 miles round trip):** The walk from the site of Washington's Headquarters to the site of the French Encampments is 3.25 miles one way. At 1.25 miles into the walk, the road to the right goes 2 miles to L, the Untouched Redoubt. So, for equal distance you can choose to go straight to the French Encampment or turn right on the road and visit the Untouched Redoubt. Parking is available at H.

Points of Interest

1. **Redoubts 9 and 10 (marked as D on the map):** On October 14, 1781, three days prior to Cornwallis' proposal of surrender, the French troops attacked Redoubt 9 and the American troops attacked Redoubt 10. Together they succeeded.

2. **Moore House (marked as E on the map):** Moore House is where the surrender was negotiated for the Siege of 1781. Cornwallis chose Moore House because it was out of the line of fire.

   Sir John Harvey, the ousted governor, first patented the Moore House land in 1631. George Ludlow acquired the land later. His nephew Lieutenant Colonel Thomas Ludlow inherited the land when George died. At that point, it was called Ludlow Plantation, but when Thomas died, his wife married Reverend Peter Temple. After that, it was called Temple Farm.

   Major Lawrence Smith owned it next. He supported Governor Berkeley against Nathaniel Bacon. But his men refused to fight fellow colonists and they defected to Bacon's side. Lawrence Smith died in 1739. His son, Robert, inherited the Moore House land. In 1769, he sold it to Augustine Moore. Moore died in 1788 and left the house to General Thomas Nelson. It had several owners until the Civil War when it was damaged. In 1881, money was appropriated by Congress to repair the house. It was repaired but not restored at that time. It was in 1931 that the Sesquicentennial Committee donated leftover money to complete an authentic restoration.

3. **Surrender Field (marked as F on the map):** Surrender Field is the spot where Cornwallis sent General Charles O'Hara to surrender for the British. The surrender led to negotiations two years later that ended the Revolutionary War.

Yorktown Historic Walk

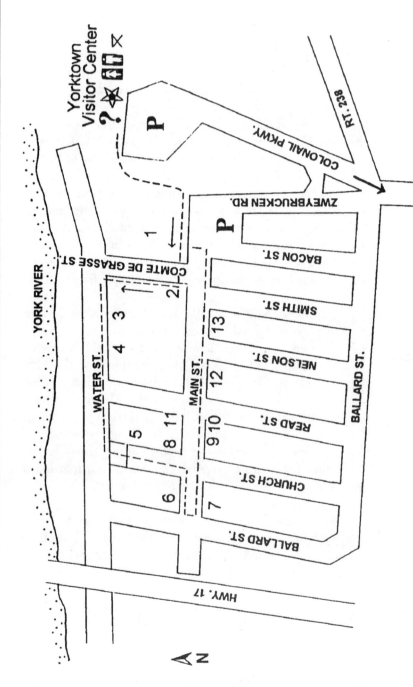

Key

?   Visitor Center

P   Parking

🛉🛉   Restrooms

- - -   Walk

✕   Picnic Area

1)   Yorktown Victory Monument

2)   Dudley Digges House

3)   Cornwallis' Cave

4)   Archer Cottage

5)   Grace Episcopal Church

6)   Courthouse

7)   Swan Tavern

8)   Somerwell House

9)   Drum Museum

10)   Custom House

11)   Pate House

12)   Nelson House

13)   Sessions House

Yorktown Historic Walk

Description

A walk through the quiet town of Yorktown on a peaceful afternoon will give you a glimpse of some of the earliest history of the country. Many historical figures responsible for the early development of the United States lived here. Soon after the area was settled, Yorktown became a busy port with importing of goods for the colonists and exporting their products for sale. On this one mile walk, you'll pass picturesque historic buildings that have been restored or still remain to mark the beginning of a nation.

Strategically located on the banks of the York River, Yorktown bustled with activity as one of the most important ports of colonial times. When port activities dwindled with the onset of the Revolutionary War, the town survived as a preferred place to live in the new nation. Yorktown survived the Siege of 1781 and the confrontation between McClellan (Union) and Magruder (Confederate) during the Civil War. Today, the National Park Service maintains the historic area of Yorktown. It is as a great place to absorb the history of the birth of a nation.

Location

To reach Yorktown from the south, use I-64 and take the J. Clyde Morris Blvd. North (Rt. 17) exit. Follow Rt. 17 to Yorktown. When you get close to Yorktown, you'll see signs for Yorktown Battlefield. Follow the signs to the Visitor Center. From the north, use I-64 and take the Yorktown exit onto the Colonial Parkway. Follow the Colonial Parkway to Yorktown and follow the signs to the Visitor Center.

Parking and Facilities

Parking, picnic areas, and restrooms are available at the Visitor Center. Parking is also available at the bottom of Comte de Grasse

Street on the York River where there is a picnic area, and there is parking at the east end of Main Street across from the Victory Monument.

Background

Yorktown wasn't established until 1691 when an "Act of Ports" stipulated the purchase of land along Tidewater waterways for establishing port towns; however, settlers saw the potential of the location on the river and settled in the area of Yorktown as early as 1620. One of these early colonists was Captain Nicolas Martiau. He arrived in the area specifically to build a fort at Yorktown. He became a member of the House of Burgesses one year later. After the Indian massacre of 1622, Martiau was assigned to build a fort at the mouth of Wormley Creek, which is 2 miles down river from the current location of Yorktown. Because the fort was such a good safeguard against attacks on the York River and because the river was deep enough to accommodate large ships, the area where Yorktown is today became an excellent location for a port.

In 1635, Martiau received a patent for 1600 acres, including the area of Yorktown. His neighbor was Sir John Harvey, Governor of the colony. Martiau and Harvey did not see eye-to-eye, and Martiau's opposition to Harvey's harsh rule of the colonists was well known. Eventually others joined Martiau's opposition, and Harvey was sent back to England. It is said that this is one of the first acts of rebellion that would later lead to independence.

In 1642, the name of the river was changed to York River in honor of the Duke of York, and Martiau continued to be one of the most influential men of the time. He is responsible for bringing others from England to the area.

After Yorktown was established in 1691, wharves were built to accommodate the shipping trade. Yorktown thrived for many years as a busy port. Tobacco was the chief product of the colonists, and many comfort items, such as silks, satins and laces, jewelry, wines, silver, etc. were imported from England through Yorktown. The area became rich and many large homes were built in the town and in the area to accommodate the influential residents of the area. The citizens of Yorktown prospered through the tobacco industry and the shipping trade. Their prosperity led them to build grand residences in Yorktown as well as plantations in the surrounding area.

Tobacco was such a booming industry that the landowners over-used the land and wore it out. The subsequent inferior tobacco crops caused the tobacco trade to slow, but the port continued to do steady business in other products and thrived until the Siege of 1781 when the Revolutionary War thwarted all business. Yorktown is probably most famous because it is here that the British surrendered in the last major battle of the Revolutionary War.

Yorktown saw activity during the Civil War, too. The town was occupied by the Union troops. The Confederates held their position against the Union army during the Peninsula Campaign of 1862 for a time, but they were outnumbered by Union troops and seeing no way to win, the Confederates eventually withdrew to Richmond to defend the Confederate capital. After each of the wars, the town was rebuilt. Today it is a quiet river town with many historic sites for the public to visit.

Walk (1 mile)

Start the walk on the walkway from the Visitor Center to the Yorktown Victory Monument. Turn right onto Comte de Grasse St. Turn left onto Water Street by Cornwallis' Cave. Continue past Read St. and go up the stairs between Read St. and Ballard St. Walk to Main St. and turn right. Proceed to Ballard Street and turn around. Walk the length of Main St. and follow the walkway back to the Visitor Center.

Points of Interest

1. **Yorktown Victory Monument:** The Yorktown Victory Monument was completed in 1884. It is actually the third monument erected to commemorate the victory at Yorktown. William Nelson is responsible for the first. It was a white marble shaft 13 feet high. It was erected in 1860 to mark where Cornwallis surrendered. It disappeared during the Civil War. Presumably, it was taken in pieces as souvenirs. The second was erected by a Mr. Shaw who was the custodian of the National Cemetery at Yorktown. This one stands 10 feet high

and is located at a spot marked by the stumps of four poplar trees planted by William Nelson.

On October 29, 1781, a resolution was passed by the first Continental Congress specifying the erection of the current monument. It was a little over 100 years, however, before the monument was completed. There are two bronze tablets on the path to the monument where the names of the French and American soldiers killed in the Siege of 1781 are recorded.

2. *Dudley Digges House:* The Dudley Digges House is a good example of a typical Tidewater house. It changed hands several times before Cole Digges bought it in 1731. His son, Dudley, inherited it in 1744. Dudley Digges was a friend of Patrick Henry and he served in the House of Burgesses for 24 years from 1752 until 1776. Digges was the Comptroller of Customs for Yorktown from 1770 until 1776, a member of the Virginia Council from 1776 until 1781, and Rector of William and May College from 1782 until 1784. The house was damaged by cannon fire in 1781 and again in 1862. It was restored to its original appearance in 1960 by the National Park Service.

3. *Cornwallis' Cave:* Although many say that this was Cornwallis' headquarters during the Siege of 1781, others say that it was used most often by British officers. Cornwallis led the British during the siege and when it came time to surrender, he pleaded illness and sent General O'Hara to surrender. Cornwallis also set up a makeshift headquarters in Grace Episcopal Church and stored his gunpowder there.

4. *Archer Cottage:* Abraham Archer was a merchant and built this house in the early 1700's. Although the fire of 1814 leveled the house, the National Park Service restored it as a good representation of the simple structures found on the waterfront.

5. *Grace Episcopal Church:* The church was originally called the York-Hampton Church. The original church was built in 1642, but only one section of the foundation wall still remains. In 1697, when the seat of York County was moved to Yorktown, the York-Hampton Church was built and became the center of

worship for the area. The first minister, Reverend Anthony Panton, was fired for criticizing the Secretary of the Colony. After that, the clergy changed frequently. In those early years, a ministry at the church was appealing to many clergy because Yorktown was such an attractive place to live.

During the Revolutionary War, the interior of the church, including the pews and the furniture, were destroyed due to the rough treatment of Cornwallis' men when they used the church to store gunpowder. After the war, the citizens restored the church. During the fire of 1814, the church was damaged again. It wasn't rebuilt until 1848, and it was renamed Grace Episcopal Church at that time. During the Civil War, the belfry was used as a lookout by the North, and the church was also used as a hospital. Also during the Civil War, the Courthouse across the street was blown up and the church was again damaged. It was rebuilt in 1926. The bell in the belfry was cast in London in 1725 and was broken in the fire of 1814. It was recast in 1882. General Thomas Nelson, Jr. who signed the Declaration of Independence, is buried in the churchyard as are 6 generations of Nelsons. Major William Gooch, who was a member of the King's Council and the House of Burgesses, is also buried here. He died in 1655, and his tombstone is the oldest in York County. Pieces of the original silver communion service are still in use at the church.

6. *Courthouse:* Before the first courthouse was built, court was held in the homes of Captain John Utie and Captain Robert Baldry. The first courthouse in Yorktown was built in 1697. In 1730, a new larger courthouse, more befitting the prosperous times, was built. During the Siege of 1781, the courthouse was held by the British. Later, the French used it as a hospital. The courthouse was used until 1814 when the fire destroyed it. It was rebuilt in 1818 and lasted until the Civil War. It was used by the Union troops to store gunpowder and was blown up in 1863. In 1876, a new courthouse was built. It was used until the present one was built.

7. *Swan Tavern:* Swan Tavern was the center of town news and entertainment because it was centrally located for both visitors

and for traders and shipmasters. The tavern was so popular that it stayed in business for 140 years. In 1706, Daniel Taylor purchased the lot for 180 pounds of tobacco. It changed hands a couple more times during the intervening years. Then in 1719, Thomas "Scotch Tom" Nelson and Joseph Walker bought it and built on the land a year or two later. In 1722, they opened the tavern. In 1742, William Nelson, eldest son of Scotch Tom, bought Walker's share, and in 1761, it went to Thomas, Jr., who was a General of the Virginia Militia during the Revolution and the third governor of the new state of Virginia. The first and second floors both consisted of 4 large rooms off a central hall. The second floor was used for lodging with 4 to 8 beds in a room. When business was brisk, people also slept on the floor. Food and liquor were served on the first floor and often there was entertainment both inside and outside the tavern. Performers would entertain inside and wrestling matches, tests of strength and cock fights often took place outside. As with all taverns of that time, public meetings were often held at Swan Tavern. In 1863, when the courthouse blew up, the tavern burned. In 1875, Samuel Brent bought the lot and built a hotel, "Brent Hotel." In 1905, it was renamed Swan Tavern, but it burned again. In 1933, the National Park Service excavated the lot and found the foundation of the old Swan Tavern. In 1935, it was restored and furnished as a museum of 18th century English antiques.

8. *Somerwell House:* Mungo Somerwell was a ferryman. He built the house sometime before 1707. In 1716, the house and lot were sold to Phillip Lightfoot who was a trader and merchant. Lightfoot owned 7 other lots in Yorktown as well as property in 8 other counties. He bought the property for an investment. Mungo had died in 1707, and the property at the time of Lightfoot's acquisition was being used as an ordinary (an inn). When Philip Lightfoot died in 1748, his son William inherited the house. He left the house to his son, Philip, who sold it to John Moss of Richmond in 1783. At one point, John Moss built a store on the property. Miraculously, the house survived the Siege of 1781, the fire of 1814, and the Civil War. In 1936, the National Park Service restored the house.

9. **Drum Museum:** The Drum Museum is the home of the Fifes and Drums of York Town. The museum displays musical instruments used in the Revolutionary War, Civil War, and World War I.

10. **Custom House:** The lot was first purchased by Captain Daniel Taylor in 1691, but he didn't build on it within a year, so he lost it. In 1706, George Burton bought the lot and built on it. In 1721, Richard Ambler, Collector of Ports, bought it and built a two story frame structure and a two story brick storehouse on the land. Later, in 1726, he bought two adjacent lots for stables and a garden. In 1863, the house was destroyed by fire, but the storehouse remains today and is know as the Custom House. It is believed to be the oldest customhouse in the country. People often congregated at the Custom House for the latest news, for the prices of tobacco, and for news as to the location of ships. In 1739, Richard Ambler married Elizabeth Jacquelin. In 1766 when he died, Ambler left the Yorktown property to his son, Edward. Today the Custom House is owned by the Comte de Grasse Chapter, Daughters of the American Revolution. They purchased the house in 1924 and restored it in 1929.

11. **Pate House:** Thomas Pate was a ferryman from Gloucester. He built the house in 1703. It was sold to the Digges family and used for rental. Today the National Park Service owns the house.

12. **Nelson House:** Thomas "Scotch Tom" Nelson bought the lot in 1706 but didn't begin to build the house until 1711. Nelson died in 1745. When his wife died in 1766, the house went to her grandson, Thomas Nelson, Jr. Thomas, Jr. was very influential in the beginning of the United States. He served in the House of Burgesses and as a member of the Continental Congresses of 1775, 1776, and 1777. He also represented York County to the Virginia Convention of 1776 and was a signer of the Declaration of Independence. Thomas, Jr. was the third governor of the new Virginia and was commanding General of the Virginia Militia. The house remained in the Nelson family until 1907 when Joseph Bryan bought it. After that, Captain George Preston Blon owned it. In 1968, it was acquired by the

National Park Service. It is a beautiful example of Georgian architecture.

13. *Sessions House:* Thomas Sessions built this house in 1692 and owned it for 9 years. It is thought to be the oldest house in Yorktown and is one of three remaining 17th century structures in York County. In 1766, Dr. Matthew Pope owned it. He was the physician to the Royal Governor and was a mayor of Yorktown twice. During the Civil War, General Negley (one of McClellan's staff) used the house as headquarters when the Federals occupied Yorktown. In 1901, Conway H. Shield, a lawyer, bought it. The house survived the Siege of 1781 and the Civil War.

Footsteps: _____

Chapter 3:
Eastern Shore

Assateague Lighthouse

Chincoteague/Assateague

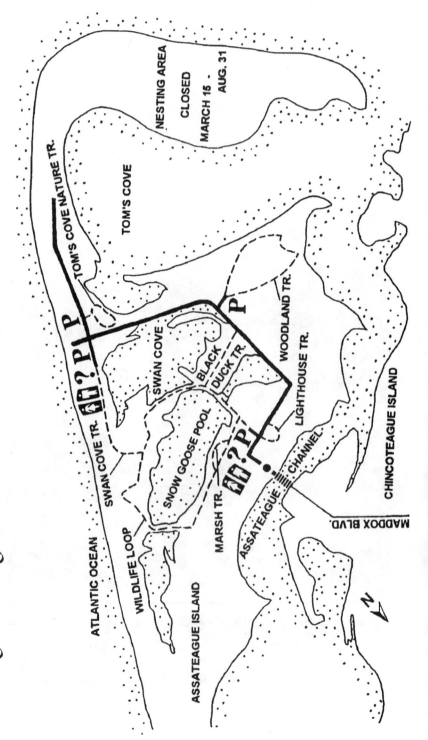

Key

- • Contact Station
- ? Visitor Center
- **P** Parking
- 🚻 Restrooms
- ▬ Park Road
- - - Trail
- ▥ Bridge

Walks

Trail	Miles
Tom's Cove Nature	0.12
Swan Cove	1.4
Wildlife Loop	3.2
Marsh	0.5
Black Duck	1.0
Lighthouse	0.25
Woodland	1.6

Eastern Shore

Chincoteague National Wildlife Refuge -- Assateague Island National Seashore

Description

A visit to the Chincoteague National Wildlife Refuge and Assateague Island National Seashore is well worth the trip up the Eastern Shore. Just driving down the main road of the refuge is a wildlife experience. Sika, Oriental elk resembling miniature deer, gather near the Refuge Headquarters, and traffic slows to a halt when geese cross Beach Road. The walks within the refuge vary in length and environments. At Tom's Cove, there are twelve miles of beach along the Atlantic Ocean to delight those who enjoy the natural environment of the Assateague Island National Seashore. There are approximately 8 miles of nature trails in the refuge. The trails vary in length from 1/8th mile to 3.25 miles. There are over 260 species of birds on the island; the most well-known are Canada geese, egret, snow geese, great blue heron, and swans. The wild ponies are also a big attraction; especially since Marguerite Henry made them famous with her book, *Misty*. The refuge trails present a variety of environments and wildlife. The contrast among the beach, the tall trees of the Woodland Trail, and the marshes of the Wildlife Loop and the many waterfowl that inhabit that area give walkers an added appreciation of the diversity and beauty of each environment. Since you've made the trip, be sure to allow enough time to try more than one walk for a complete nature experience within the refuge. As the Chincoteague National Wildlife Refuge was originally established to preserve a wintering area for migratory waterfowl, this location is a must for birders.

Location

Chincoteague National Wildlife Refuge and Assateague Island National Seashore are located on the Eastern Shore of Virginia. To reach them from I-64, take Northampton Blvd. (Rt. 13). Follow Northampton Blvd (Rt. 13) over the Chesapeake Bay Bridge Tunnel. Currently, each car must pay a toll. Continue to follow Rt. 13 until you reach Rt. 175 outside Oak Hall. Take Rt. 175 toward Chincoteague and follow the signs to Chincoteague. Once you cross the bridge over the Chincoteague Bay onto the island, turn left on Main Street then right onto Maddox Blvd., which will take you out to the Chincoteague Refuge Headquarters. There is a fee at the Contact Station at the entrance to the refuge.

Parking and Facilities

Parking is available at the Chincoteague Refuge Headquarters, Lighthouse Trail, Woodland Trail, and at Tom's Cove Visitor Center. Assateague Island National Seashore information is available at Tom's Cove Visitor Center. Restrooms are available at the Chincoteague Refuge Headquarters and at the bath house at Tom's Cove.

Background

The first visitors to Chincoteague were Indians. There is no definitive evidence that they lived on Chincoteague Island. Instead, it is thought that they used the island for hunting. It is also believed, from descriptions of the places he landed, that Verrazzano was the first explorer to land at Chincoteague. In 1524, he left France and sailed to the new world. He first landed at Cape Fear in North Carolina. From there, he sailed north and landed in a place he called Arcadia. Chincoteague is believed to be Arcadia. Because he landed on a barrier island, he was prevented from exploring inland. Therefore, Verrazzano didn't stay long. From Arcadia, he sailed farther north to what is now the New York Harbor.

Henry Norwood was one of the first to interact with the Chincoteague Indians for whom the island is named. When Norwood and 18 others were marooned on the Delmarva Peninsula in 1650, they were rescued by the Kicotanks. Though communication with the Indians was difficult, Norwood finally made it known that he wanted to find the English settlement Accomack on the Eastern Shore. Kicotank summoned a guide to take Norwood to Accomack. On their way, Norwood and the others stayed at the village of the Chincoteague Indians.

In 1664, the land surrounding Chincoteague Creek was patented by Englishmen. Where NASA is now became the property of John

Wallop (south bank), and Edmund Scarburgh claimed the north bank which consisted of 3,000 acres. Because Scarburgh was unfriendly to the Indians, the Chincoteague Indians abandoned their home and moved north away from the attacks by Scarburgh.

On January 20, 1680, Thomas Welburn and four of his employees crossed the Chincoteague Bay from the mainland and laid claim to Chincoteague Island. Welburn's tenant, Robert Scott, was the first inhabitant of the island. He stayed for one year.

Although Welburn considered Chincoteague Island to be his, his patent was never seated, so a new patent was issued in 1684 to John Clayton. After that, John Clayton's patent next went to Colonel William Kendall who was speaker of the House of Burgesses. But Welburn still considered the island to be his and threatened to shoot anyone on the island.

In 1686, Kendall armed himself in case of an attack by Welburn and built a small house on the island. Instead of settling the matter with gunfire, Welburn finally decided to take Kendall to court. Both wanted the island for pasture for their livestock rather than a place to build a residence. The case took three years, and in the end, Kendall won.

In 1686, Henry Towles, was the first man to live on the island and own the land, too. He started as a guard for Kendall and eventually bought some land from him. Towles lived there until 1709.

No one knows for sure the origin of the wild ponies of Assateague. The legend and most glamorous story is that a Spanish galleon with a load of mustangs was shipwrecked off the island during the 1700s and the ponies made it to shore. Another is that landowners on the mainland found it cheaper to keep their livestock on the island when laws were passed that all livestock must be fenced, and that the ponies are descendants of this stock. Regardless of the true story, today the ponies are a big attraction of the area. There are two herds -- one in Maryland and another in Virginia. The book, *Misty*, by Marguerite Henry and later the movie have made these ponies famous. On the Virginia side, the herd is rounded up on Assateague and forced to swim the Assateague Channel to Chincoteague in

July. They are then sold at auction and the profits are used by the owners of the ponies, the Chincoteague Volunteer Fire Department. The event always draws a big crowd.

During the Revolutionary War, the islanders and those owning land joined the American cause. British ships blocked the Chesapeake Bay; therefore, ships began to land on the Eastern Shore during the war years. Because this area became a vital shipping harbor, Chincoteague was fortified in 1776 and a fort was built on the mainland.

Between the Revolutionary War and the Civil War, the seafood industry of the area took off. Before this, farming was the main enterprise. Today, seafood is still the main industry with oysters as the biggest part of that industry. Clams are second and fish, including trout, croaker, and spot, are third.

Chincoteague distinguished itself during the Civil War. In 1861, when Virginia seceded from the Union, only two areas --Tangier Island and Chincoteague Island -- chose not to secede.

After the war, work that started in 1857 to replace the out-of-date Assateague Lighthouse was completed to prevent the frequent shipwrecks. But with increased trade, shipwrecks continued. Soon after that, the Life-Saving Service was established. In 1875, two stations were established on Assateague Island -- one of them was located at Tom's Cove.

It is interesting how nature and erosion have made changes to the island over the years. In 1866, Tom's Cove wasn't there at all. The channel between Assateague and Chincoteague was much narrower, too. Erosion eventually widened the waterway by narrowing Chincoteague.

In 1943, Nellie Field Burwell sold 8,000 acres which included the whole of the Virginia portion of Assateague Island National Seashore to the government and the Chincoteague National Wildlife Refuge was established to provide a wintering area for migratory waterfowl. Today, the Fish and Wildlife Service, U.S. Department of the Interior manages the Chincoteague National Wildlife Refuge, and the National Park Service, U.S. Department of the Interior manages Assateague Island National Seashore. The U.S. Department of the Interior is devoted to preserving the area as a coastal habitat for the birds and wildlife.

Walks

1. **Tom's Cove Nature Trail (1/8 mile):** To those of you who are avid walkers, 1/8th of a mile is barely a walk. This trail is included, however, because, in that short distance, the trail demonstrates three environments: interdune, salt marsh, and shrub thicket. This walk gives you a taste of the habitats important to the survival of the beach.

2. **Beach Walk (12 miles):** The Tom's Cove Visitor Center is a good starting point for a beach walk. There are 12 miles of beach environment to enjoy. On the walk, you'll see shore birds and evidence of many forms of sea life, including horseshoe crabs, fiddler crabs, shells, as well as dunes and beach vegetation. Keep track of the distance you go and turn around with enough energy left to return to where you parked.

3. **Swan Cove Trail (1.25 miles):** The Swan Cove Trail starts to the left of Tom's Cove Visitor Center as you face the ocean. The trail follows the beach then turns inland and proceeds to the Wildlife Loop. The Swan Cove Trail is 1.25 miles one way. When you reach the Wildlife Loop, you can turn around and return to where you parked or combine it with the Wildlife Loop which is 3.25 miles.

4. **Wildlife Loop (3.25 miles):** This trail begins and ends at the Chincoteague Refuge Visitor Center/Headquarters. The Wildlife Loop gives you a scenic view of the marsh and of Snow Goose Pool. You'll see waterfowl in abundance on this trail. It is not uncommon to see Canada geese or a great egret feeding in the shallows of Snow Goose Pool. The loop is open to walk and bike, and from 3pm until dusk, it is open to vehicles.

5. **Marsh Trail (.5 miles):** Marsh Trail is a half mile trail within the Wildlife Loop. It cuts in for a closer look at Snow Goose

Pool. The overlook at the pool is a great place to stop and enjoy the waterfowl and wildlife.

6. *Lighthouse Trail (.25 miles):* This is a short quarter mile trail, but it's worth a look. It will take you to the Assateague Lighthouse. The view from beside the lighthouse is spectacular.

7. *Black Duck Trail (1 mile):* This trail is another way to reach the Wildlife Loop. It goes from Beach Road to the Wildlife Loop.

8. *Woodland Trail (1.6 miles):* This trail is open to walkers and to bikers. Tall trees line the trail, and partway through the trail is an overlook. It's likely that you'll see wild ponies from this vantage point.

Footsteps: _____

Beaverdam Park

Beaverdam Park

YOUTH CAMPGROUND

HIKING TRAIL

BEAVERDAM LAKE

LOOP 4

LOOP 3

LOOP 2

LOOP 1

P

EXERCISE TRAIL

ROUTE 616

N

Walks

Trail	Miles	Trail Markers
Loop 1	0.5	Blue
Loop 2	1.0	Red
Loop 3	2.0	Yellow
Loop 4	3.5	Orange

Key

? Ranger Station

P Parking

🚻 Restrooms

✪ Start Here

- - - - Nature Trail

==== Hiking Trail

✕ Picnic Area

▓▓▓ Bridge/Earthen Crossover

Footsteps: _____
Beaverdam Park

Description

Although Beaverdam Park, on the outskirts of Gloucester, is a ways off the beaten path, it's well worth the trip. Flocks of Canada geese stop here on their way south, and it's easy to see why. In constructing the park, every effort has been made to preserve the natural beauty and integrity of the environment. The nature trail is carved into the banks of the Beaverdam Reservoir. Throughout the lowland portion of the trail, you'll skirt the shore of the lake with a breathtaking view of the lake and the wetland environment. On the backside of the trail, you'll catch glimpses of the lake; but, for most of the highland portion of the trail, you may feel as if you've been transported back in time and dropped into a colonial wilderness. Numerous benches have been placed strategically along the trail to provide rest and picturesque spots to enjoy the scenery and observe the many varieties of wildlife. It is not uncommon to see great blue heron, wood ducks, and osprey as well as turtles near the lake. The park is also home to bald eagles. The nature trail has four distinct loops, so you can devise a nature walk as short as .5 miles or as long as 3.5 miles.

Location
Main Entrance
Beaverdam Park is located on the outskirts of Gloucester. To reach the park from the south, take I- 64 to Rt. 17- J. Clyde Morris Blvd. toward Yorktown. Follow Rt. 17 across the Coleman Bridge at Yorktown. Continue on Rt. 17 to Gloucester, bearing right onto Rt. 17 - Business. Go through the town of Gloucester and turn right onto Roaring Springs Road (Rt. 616). Follow Roaring Springs Road to the end and you will be at the park.

To reach the main entrance from the north, take I-64 to Fort Eustis Blvd. - Rt.105 toward Yorktown. Follow Fort Eustis Blvd. to Rt.

17. Turn left onto Rt. 17. Follow Rt. 17 across the Coleman Bridge at Yorktown. Continue on Rt. 17 to Gloucester bearing right onto Rt. 17 - Business. Go through the town of Gloucester and turn right onto Roaring Springs Road (Rt. 616). Follow Roaring Springs Road to the end and you will be at the park.

Alternate Entrance
There is an entrance to another portion of the park at the opposite end of Beaverdam Reservoir. At this entrance, there is a 3 mile multi-use trail. To reach the alternate entrance, follow Rt. 17 to Ark Road (Rt. 606). Turn right onto Rt. 606 and follow it 2.5 miles to the alternate entrance. Turn right into the entrance.

Parking and Facilities
There are large parking areas at both entrances. There are also restroom facilities at both entrances. The park also has picnic areas, a boat ramp, boat, paddle boat and canoe rentals, and a youth camping area. The park is open by 8:00 a.m. daily and closes at sunset.

Background
Beaverdam Park is managed by the Gloucester County Parks and Recreation Department. Originally, the area consisted of three streams cutting through open fields, wetlands, and woods. In 1990, the area was flooded, creating a 635 acre reservoir that provides the water supply for the surrounding area. Despite the care taken, flooding the area temporarily disturbed the natural habitat of the many varieties of birds, animals, insects, and reptiles indigenous to the area. Fortunately, most of them have resettled, and all the original wetlands have been re-established.

Currently, there is the 3.5 mile nature trail at the main entrance portion of the park with a 1.3 mile extension that is known as a hiking trail into a rustic youth campground. In addition, there is a three mile multi-purpose trail for hiking, biking, jogging, and horseback riding at the alternate entrance. Park rangers maintain the well-groomed trails and members of local trail and bike associations assist with trail construction and maintenance a couple of times a year. Other trails in Beaverdam Park are still in the planning/construction stage. Eventually, there will be 22 miles of wilderness trails surrounding the lake.

Footsteps:

Walk

There is a trail marker at the entrance to the nature trail. The total length (out and back) of the nature trail is 3.5 miles. There are four loops that are marked as follows:

Loop 1 (blue markers) = .5 miles
Loop 2 (red markers) = 1 mile
Loop 3 (yellow markers) = 2 miles
Loop 4 (orange markers) = 3.5 miles.

The mileage for each loop includes how far you will walk if you go to the end of any given loop and walk back to the entrance to the trail. The highland portion of the trail is marked entirely in orange markers. Loop colors are painted on trees along the trail, so you can decide how far you want to go and crossover to the highland portion of the trail at the end of a loop to return to the trail entrance. If you walk all four loops of the trail, you'll encounter three earthen crossovers/bridges. These are grassy paths formed to bridge the fingers of the reservoir. Throughout the trail, markers point out plants and trees of interest. Numbers on these markers correspond to the guidebook available at the Ranger Station. The trial is wide and well-maintained but be prepared for hilly terrain on both the lowland and the highland portions of the trail.

Points of Interest

1. **Boat Ramp and Pier:** Rental of paddle boats, canoes, or boats can be arranged at the Ranger Station at the main entrance to Beaverdam Park. In addition, there is a public boat ramp if you wish to put your own boat in the water. A yearly boat/canoe permit is required to use your own boat. Permits for boating/canoeing are available at the Ranger Station as are fishing and hunting licenses. There are many varieties of fish in the lake and there are 11 marked fish attractors. There is also a boat ramp at the alternate entrance off Route 606. It is for those patrons who have annual passes.

2. **Exercise Trail:** On the other side of the parking lot from the nature trail is a Gamefield Jogging Course. This consists of 20 creative fitness events and 5 health education stations. For a

complete workout, combine jogging on Loop 1 of the nature trail with this exercise course.

3. *Hiking Trail:* The hiking trail begins at the far end of Loop 4 of the nature trail. It leads 1.3 miles to the youth camping area. At .2 miles into the hiking trail, from the juncture with Loop 4, is a wooden bridge. To the right side of the bridge, you can see lodges built by the beavers. If you want to add distance to your walk, you can go out and back on the hiking trail, which will bring the total mileage of your walk to approximately 6 miles.

4. *Camping:* There is a youth campground at the end of the hiking trail. The only way to reach the campground is to hike to it by following the nature trail to the end of Loop 4 then bearing to the left down the hiking trail. Reservations are required to camp. Information regarding camping is available at the Ranger Station.

5. *Multi-purpose Trail:* The multi-purpose trail is located at the alternate entrance off Route 606. It is designed for walking, jogging, biking, and horseback riding and is about 3 miles in length.

6. *Picnic Areas:* There is a picnic shelter at the main entrance that accommodates large groups. Reservations can be arranged through the Ranger Station. In addition, there are numerous picnic tables and grills throughout the main entrance area.

Gloucester

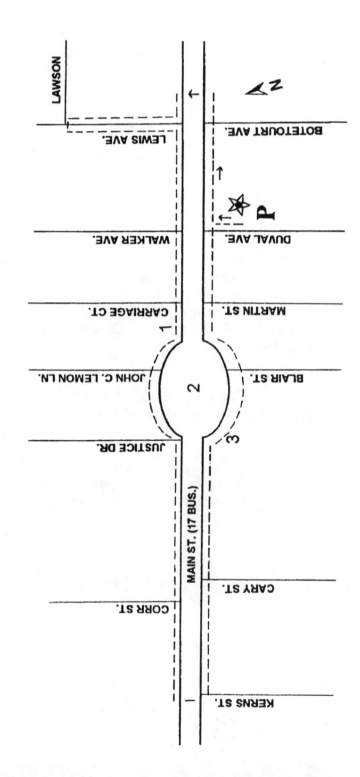

Key

P Parking

🛉🛊 Restrooms

✪ Start Here

– – – Walk

1) Hotel Botetourt
2) Courthouse Square
3) Botetourt Lodge

Gloucester

Description

The residents of Gloucester are proud of their history and have taken great pains to preserve the atmosphere of the past. Main Street Gloucester is less than one mile long, but that short distance is packed with excellent examples of early American architecture and history. The history of Gloucester County dates back to colonial days, and the Gloucester historic walk offers an opportunity to learn about the area while strolling through this remarkable town. In the span of 1.5 miles, this historic walk will take you the length of the town and back, highlighting the Courthouse District. Allow plenty of time to pause and enjoy the many historic landmarks along the way.

Location

To reach Gloucester from the south, take I-64 to Rt. 17- J. Clyde Morris Blvd. toward Yorktown. Follow Rt. 17 across the Coleman Bridge at Yorktown. Continue on Rt. 17 to Gloucester, bearing right onto Rt. 17 Business.

To reach Gloucester from the north, take I-64 to Fort Eustis Blvd. - Rt. 105 toward Yorktown. Follow Fort Eustis Blvd. to Rt. 17. Turn left onto Rt. 17. Follow Rt. 17 across the Coleman Bridge at Yorktown. Continue on Rt. 17 to Gloucester, bearing right onto Rt. 17- Business.

Parking and Facilities

Turn left onto Duval Avenue from Main Street (Business Route 17) and park on the right side of Duval Avenue in the public parking area. The Courthouse District buildings are open to the public on weekdays between 8:00 a.m. and 4:30 p.m. You can walk around the buildings at courthouse square any time.

Background

Early settlers arrived in the Gloucester area in 1607, shortly after Jamestown was established. In 1651, the area we now know as Gloucester County separated from York County, just across the York River. The Gloucester County Courthouse was built in 1766. It wasn't until 1769, however, that the general assembly named Gloucester, the county seat, as a town. At that time, the town of Gloucester was named Botetourt, but the name wasn't popular with the citizens, and the town became known as Gloucester.

In 1676, Nathanial Bacon pressed the residents of the Gloucester area for men and supplies for his cause, known as Bacon's Rebellion, to unseat and wrest the power from Governor Berkeley. He met resistance to his demands for men to fight on his side, but he took their supplies and left the area. The men of Gloucester traveled to Green Spring, Governor Berkeley's country home, to complain to him about Bacon's activities and the fact that he left them with very few supplies with which to defend themselves. Berkeley, too, tried to convince the men from Gloucester to ride with him against Bacon, but they were not interested in fighting other colonists. Berkeley returned to Jamestown and found the town occupied by 800 of Bacon's men. Berkeley offered them a pardon to switch sides. They accepted. When Bacon heard of the surrender of his men to Berkeley's offer of a pardon, he was once again near Gloucester. He rallied what supporters he could and returned to Jamestown. Bacon won the confrontation in Jamestown but at a great price. In the process, he burned Jamestown to the ground and Berkeley fled. The civil war that Bacon instigated, fell apart when he died of disease that same year on the Eastern Shore.

Walk

The walk starts from the parking area on Duval Avenue. Turn right onto Main Street and walk to the garden shop. Cross the street at the garden shop and proceed left up Main Street. Continue on Main Street to Lewis and turn right. Walk along Lewis Street and enjoy the scenery of the neighborhood to Lawson Street then turn around and return to Main Street. Turn right onto Main Street and walk toward the Courthouse District. When you reach the Courthouse District, you will pass the former Botetourt Hotel, which is an excellent example of a colonial hostelry (an inn). It was originally built in 1770 and restored two hundred years later to serve as a county office building. To your right, you will see several small structures. These are original buildings. The one marked with a "Real Estate" sign dates back to the early 19th century. It was the Shackelford's Saddlery Shop and is still owned by a descendent of Mr. Shackelford. As you walk around the courthouse circle, take time to cross the street and explore the historic buildings on the square. After you finish exploring, continue around the circle and up Main Street to Kerns Street and cross Main Street at the Botetourt School crosswalk. Turn left and follow Main Street back toward the Courthouse District. Bear right when you reach the circle. On your right will be the Botetourt Lodge and commercial area. The smaller buildings are examples of simple structures from the mid - 19th and 20th centuries. This was the commercial area of the old town. Today, they house law and commercial offices. Continue around the circle and return on Main Street to the parking area. Be sure to take time to stop in the many little shops (eateries, book stores and antique shops) along the way on either side of the street.

Points of Interest

1. *Hotel Botetourt:* On the circle across the street from the court-house, you will see the Hotel Botetourt. It was built about the time that Gloucester was named the county seat. This is an example of a pre-Revolutionary hostelry and welcomed visitors for about 200 years. The residents of Gloucester bought the structure in 1965 and restored it. It was awarded the Preservation of Virginia Antiquities Award for Historic Preservation in 1971 and is now used as the county administrative office building.

2. *Gloucester County Courthouse Square*
    Courthouse: The courthouse, built in 1766, was a working courthouse for the county until 1982 when the new building opened. Within the courthouse are numerous memorial plaques and tablets honoring men and women of the area, such as Walter Reed (the discoverer of the cause of yellow fever) and Nathaniel Bacon (of Bacon's Rebellion fame), for their contributions to the area and to humanity.

Debtor's Prison: The Debtor's Prison was built in 1810. It was used for approximately 40 years to house debtors. Later, it was used as an arsenal during the Civil War.

The Jail: The original jail burned during the Civil War. It was rebuilt on the same location in 1873. It provides an example of post-war architecture.

The Clayton Building: This building, too, was destroyed by fire. It was rebuilt in 1823 and served as the clerk's office. It was named for John Clayton who was the clerk of the Gloucester court from 1720 to 1773. He was the son of John Clayton who was attorney-general of the colony of Virginia.

The Roane Building: This building was named for Basil Roane who served as deputy clerk and clerk of the Circuit Court. The Roan Building was built in 1896.

The Confederate Monument: The monument was built in 1889 as a memorial to the men who lost their lives in the Civil War. It stands in the center of the courthouse circle and lists the names of 132 men.

3. *Botetourt Lodge:* This Masonic Hall is on the edge of the Courthouse District and was the location of the Lodge No. 7 from 1757.

Points of Interest in the Vicinity

Although the Courthouse District garners most of the attention of visitors, there are a couple of other points of interest you shouldn't miss. They are Ware Church and the Long Bridge Ordinary. They are accessible by car on the way into Gloucester.

1. *Long Bridge Ordinary:* The Long Bridge Ordinary is located on your right at the intersection of Main Street and John Clayton Memorial Highway as you drive into town. An "ordinary" was the predecessor to our motels. Travelers could have a meal on the main floor then rent one of the cots lined up in the room on the second floor. The Long Bridge Ordinary was built in the 18th century. The original structure consisted of

one room with a side passage structure. The porches and other areas were added later. It was known as Edge Hill during the 19th century. It was purchased by the Gloucester's Woman's Club in 1923 and is still used by that organization.

2. ***Ware Church:*** As you drive into town, turn right onto John Clayton Memorial Highway and look for Ware Church one mile on your right from the intersection with Main Street. The construction date of the church is unknown, but it is thought to have been built sometime around 1660, then after a fire was rebuilt across the river from the original church sometime between 1710 and 1750. It is Virginia's only rectangular colonial church served by 3 entrances. It was abandoned at one point, but now is occupied by Episcopalians. It is a beautiful structure. Be sure to walk around back where an old cemetery sits beneath tall trees.

Chapter 5:
Hampton

Fort Monroe

Fort Monroe

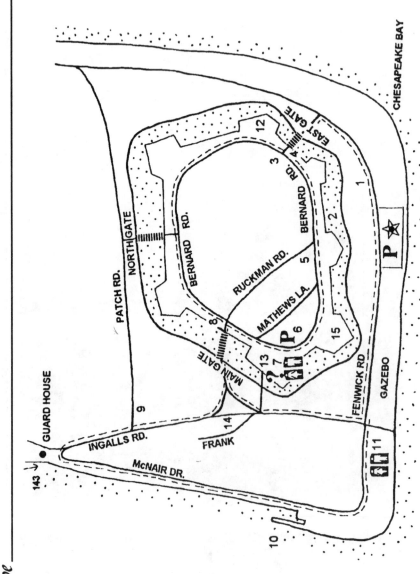

Key

? Visitor Center

P Parking

🚻 Restrooms

⭐ Start Here

- - - Walk

▓▓▓ Bridge

1) Lighthouse
2) Moat
3) Quarters
4) Incline
5) Chapel of the Centurion
6) Lee's Quarters
7) Casemate Museum

8) Stockade
9) Arsenal
10) Marina
11) Chamberlin Hotel
12) Battery Gatewood
13) Postern Bridge
14) St. Mary Star of the Sea
15) Flagstaff Bastion

Description

Fort Monroe, the largest stone fort built in the United States, is located on the Hampton side of the Hampton Roads Bridge-Tunnel. The original architecture, dating from the pre-civil war era to the present, makes this a unique walk with many points of interest. One of the first sites you'll see is the working lighthouse that overlooks the Chesapeake Bay. Once inside the fort, you can choose a walk that takes in the many buildings of historical significance or a walk on the top of the fort wall that offers a breathtaking view of the surrounding area. Both walks are enhanced by a variety of southern blooming flowers, trees, and bushes.

Location

To reach Fort Monroe, take I-64 to 169 East - Mallory Street. At the end of the exit ramp, turn left onto Mallory (169). Continue on Mallory Street to Mellen (143). Turn right onto Mellen (143 E) and head toward Fort Monroe. Stay on this road approximately ½ mile. You'll see the guard house for the base ahead. Bear right onto McNair Drive and follow it past the marina and bear left at Fenwick. Drive past the gazebo and park in the parking area on the right.

Parking and Facilities

Parking is available on Fenwick facing the Chesapeake Bay just past the gazebo. This is where the walks described below start. In addition, parking is available in a lot near the East Gate, and you can also parallel park on Bernard Road. There are restrooms and a gift shop in the Casemate Museum. And there is a snack bar at the YMCA which is near the Main Gate. Fort Monroe is a working fort, so there are no special hours when it is closed. The Casemate Museum is open daily.

Safety Tips

1. This is a low traffic area. Sidewalks are intermittent on each of these walks. Traffic is minimal in this area but be sure to walk facing traffic and exercise caution.

2. This is a military base, so not all areas are open to the public. The Arsenal, for example, is not open to visitors, and the residence at the East Gate and Lee's Quarters are private residences and are not open to the public.

3. Most of the walk is on smooth pavement. The exception to this is the portion on the fort wall. The walking surface is mostly grassy with remnants of weapons' mountings. It is for this reason that the fort wall is not a good place to walk with strollers or wheelchairs. Additionally, we recommend that you keep children close at hand to prevent falls.

Background

Fort Monroe (Old Point Comfort) dates back to the days of the colonists. When the colonists first came to Virginia, they built their homes first, then they built a fort facing the ocean to protect their new community. On April 26, 1607, three ships (the Susan Constant, the Godspeed, and the Discovery) chartered by King James I landed at Cape Henry. For four days, a party explored the surrounding area for the most appropriate point of defense. They found and named Cape Comfort (later named Point Comfort) at the juncture of the York and James Rivers. For a few more days, they used this area as a location while they continued to explore for a location for a more permanent settlement. In May, they decided to make their settlement at Jamestown.

By the end of two years, Jamestown had expanded sufficiently that additional protection of the James River appeared necessary. In 1609, sixteen men, who arrived with Captain James Davis from England, and additional men from Jamestown were sent to build a new fort at Point Comfort.

In 1818, the importance of Old Point Comfort was re-emphasized and construction of Fort Monroe on the site was begun in 1819. Due to its strategic location at the entrances to these rivers and the

Footsteps:

Chesapeake Bay, Fort Monroe has played a significant role throughout history.

During the Civil War, Fort Monroe was nicknamed the Freedom Fort. In 1861, three black slaves ran away from their landowners and sought refuge at Fort Monroe. The guard at the gate let them in and Major General Benjamin Butler refused to return them to their owners. Word spread and approximately 300 more runaway slaves showed up for assistance. Eventually, two Black regiments were started and they built homes in the area.

For a good period of the Civil War, Fort Monroe was the only outpost within the Confederacy occupied by Union forces. At the end of the Civil War, Confederate President Jefferson Davis was jailed at Fort Monroe after his capture on May 10, 1865.

Today, Fort Monroe is the headquarters of the US Army Training and Doctrine Command. As a National Historic Landmark, Fort Monroe receives many visitors. It was named in honor of President James Monroe and is the only active fort in the country that is circled by a moat.

Walks

We have described 3 possible walks (two 2 mile walks and one 3.5 miles in length). Depending on your energy level on the day of your walk, you can use these as examples and devise your own version.

1. *Fort Walk (2 miles):* This route is approximately 2 miles long and stays on the street-level of the fort. Follow the map to the East Gate and walk over the moat and through the tunnel. Turn left onto Bernard Road. Walk around the perimeter of the fort on Bernard Road 1 ½ times until you reach the Main Gate (for the second time). Walk through the tunnel and over the moat. Bear to the left onto Ingalls Road and take a left onto Fenwick. Walk past the gazebo and return to the parking area.

2. *Fort Wall Walk (2 miles):* This route is also approximately 2 miles in length. Follow route 1 through the tunnel to Bernard

Road and turn left onto Bernard. Immediately after turning onto Bernard Road, take a sharp left up the incline to the fort wall. Walk the perimeter of the wall until you make a complete circle. Walk down the incline to the road level. Continue to the left of the incline on Bernard to the Main Gate, passing the chapel, Lee's Quarters and the entrance to the museum. Go through the tunnel and over the moat. Bear left onto Ingalls Road and take a left onto Fenwick. Walk past the gazebo and return to the parking area.

3. *Combination Fort and Fort Wall Walk (3.5 miles):* This route is approximately 3.5 miles in length. Follow route 1 to Bernard Road. Turn left onto Bernard and circle the perimeter of the fort on Bernard Road. Go past the East Gate again and walk up the incline (sharp left) just after the East Gate. Walk the perimeter of the fort wall until you reach the incline again. Walk down the incline to the road level. Continue to the left of the incline on Bernard to the Main Gate, passing the chapel, Lee's Quarters, and the entrance to the museum. Walk through the tunnel and over the moat. Bear to the right onto Ingalls Road and follow it to the guard house. Take the cut-through just before the guard house to McNair Drive and turn left. Follow McNair Drive past the marina to the Chamberlin Hotel. Turn left onto Fenwick and follow it back to the parking area.

Points of Interest:

1. *Lighthouse:* When walking from the parking area, you will pass the Old Point Comfort Lighthouse. It was built in 1802 and has continued in operation since that time.

2. *Moat:* A moat surrounds the fort. When you enter the East Gate, you will cross over the moat. It is eight feet deep. At the East Gate, it is 60 feet wide and at the Main Gate it is 150 feet wide.

3. *Quarters:* Directly in front of you when you enter the East Gate is the residence where visitors stayed. Abraham Lincoln stayed here.

4. **Incline:** For the walks on the fort wall, the incline near the East Gate is marked as 4 on the map. These inclines were used for many years to move artillery up to and down from the fort wall.

5. **Chapel of the Centurion:** The principal contributor for building the Chapel of the Centurion was Lieutenant Julian McAllister. Three years before the chapel was built, McAllister and two others were involved in an accident in the laboratory of the Arsenal. The explosion killed the others, and McAllister's contribution to the building of the chapel was in recognition of the Divine intervention in his miraculously surviving the explosion.

6. **Lee's Quarters:** Robert E. Lee was stationed at Fort Monroe from 1831 to 1834. He was a lieutenant during that time and designed buildings, wharves, and fortifications. He lived in the quarters on the right just after the Chapel of the Centurion.

7. **Casemate Museum:** As you circle Bernard Road, the Casemate Museum is on your left. It contains many interesting historical displays. Of particular note is the cell of Confederate President Jefferson Davis. When the Confederacy fell, Davis was captured on May 10, 1865 near Irwinville, Georgia. From there, he was eventually sent to Savannah then was taken by boat to Hilton Head, South Carolina. Then he was put on another boat and brought to Hampton Roads. On May 22nd, he was brought into Fort Monroe and imprisoned in Casemate No. 2. In October, he was moved to Carroll Hall due to poor health. Carroll Hall is no longer standing but the site of the hall is just past the Main Gate.

8. **Stockade:** The tunnel walk-thru at the Main Gate is the site of the stockade where prisoners were confined. They housed 20 to 40 prisoners in the main part of the tunnel with individual cells through the marked doorway.

9. **Arsenal:** If you take the longer walk that goes up Ingalls and back by way of McNair, you will pass the Fort Monroe Arsenal

that was built just before the Civil War. It is located on the right side of Ingalls Road near the intersection with Patch Road.

10. *Marina:* When driving into Fort Monroe and on the longer walk, you will pass the marina on your right on McNair.

11. *Chamberlin Hotel:* The first hotel on this site was called the Hygeia. It was built in 1820 and was known for a visit from Edgar Allan Poe, who recited "The Raven" and "Annabel Lee" from its veranda in 1849. Also of note is that it was used as a hospital during the Civil War. It was torn down in 1862. Soon thereafter, another Hygeia was built and operated as a resort. In 1894, the Chamberlin Hotel was built beside it. The Hygeia and the Chamberlin operated next to each other until 1902 when the Hygeia was torn down. The current Chamberlin Hotel was built in 1928. On your walk, it is located at the intersection of Fenwick and Ingalls Road. The Chamberlin is a beautiful structure. It has a dining room that overlooks the Chesapeake Bay and a swimming pool and tennis courts also on the bay side.

12. *Battery Gatewood:* This artillery battery is one of the oldest on the coast. When walking the fort wall, it's worth the walk up a few steps at this point for a nice view of the Chesapeake Bay.

13. *Postern Bridge:* Near the main entrance to the Casemate Museum, you may want to take a little detour through the Postern Gate. It leads to a walkway over the moat.

14. *St. Mary Star of the Sea Catholic Church:* This is one of several working churches on the base. It is just outside the Main Gate to Fort Monroe.

15. *Flagstaff Bastion:* There is an overlook at the flagpole on the fort wall. Through the telescope, you'll get a good view of the Chesapeake Bay and surrounding area. From this point, you can clearly see Fort Wool directly ahead in the bay. Fort Wool was built on a man-made island prior to the Civil War. The "Miss Hampton" Harbor Cruise, which leaves from the dock at the Chamberlin Hotel, stops at Fort Wool for a tour. Fort

Wool also can be reached by Hampton Harbor Cruises which leave from the pier near the Radisson Hotel in Hampton on Settlers Road. Fort Wool is rich in history of its own. Several presidents (Andrew Jackson, John Tyler, and Abraham Lincoln) visited the fort. Andrew Jackson used it as a favorite spot for respite, and Abraham Lincoln watched from the fort as federal troops attempted to retake Norfolk.

Grandview Nature Preserve

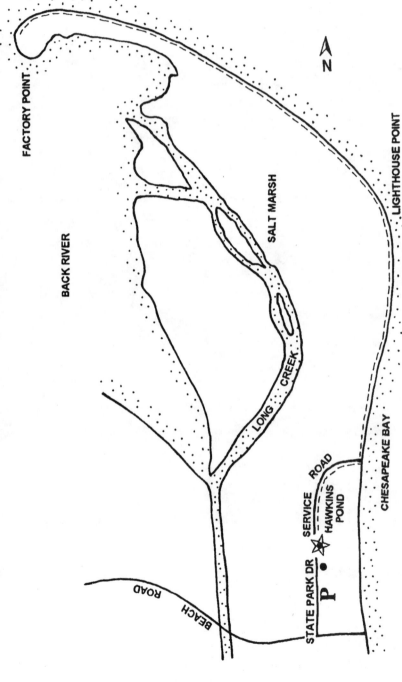

FACTORY POINT

BACK RIVER

SALT MARSH

LIGHTHOUSE POINT

LONG CREEK

CHESAPEAKE BAY

SERVICE ROAD

HAWKINS POND

STATE PARK DR

P

BEACH ROAD

N

Key

- • Park Entrance
- **P** Parking
- ☆ Start Here
- - - - Trail

Grandview Nature Preserve

Description

Grandview Nature Preserve offers a 2 ½ mile beach walk along the shore of the Chesapeake Bay. The park is an excellent spot for observation of beach wildlife and plant life and is used often by bird watching clubs and by local colleges for ecological studies. As you follow the shoreline along the beach, you will encounter a variety of seashells and horseshoe crab shells washed up on the shore, sandpipers running in and out of the surf, and sand crabs scurrying from spot to spot on the dry portions of the sand. With the bay lapping at the shore on one side and the dunes and salt marsh on the other, this is a picturesque setting for a walk. Be sure to bring binoculars to observe the many varieties of waterfowl and shore birds that live in this area. As you near Factory Point, you'll walk along a sliver of land where the Chesapeake Bay meets Back River, offering a panoramic view of the surrounding waters.

Location

Grandview Nature Preserve is located in Hampton. To reach it from I-64, take the Mercury Blvd. - Route 258 North exit. Follow Mercury Blvd. and watch for Fox Hill Road. Turn left onto Fox Hill Road (not Old Fox Hill Road) and watch for Beach Road. Turn Left onto Beach Road and follow it to State Park Drive. Turn left onto State Park Drive.

Parking and Facilities

Parallel parking is available on State Park Drive near the entrance to Grandview Nature Preserve. Parking is prohibited in this area between sunset and 7:00 a.m.; therefore, be sure to leave the beach area in plenty of time to reach your car before dark. This is an unmanned area. There are no services and no restrooms. Visit Grandview Nature Preserve during daylight only. The park opens at sunrise and closes at sunset.

Safety Tips

1. It is advisable to walk at low tide as the beach narrows against the sand dunes in several places.

2. No open fires are allowed in the park.

3. No dogs are allowed in the park during nesting season between April through September.

Background

Grandview Nature Preserve is a 578 acre park managed by the Hampton Department of Parks and Recreation. It was established in 1970 after the city of Hampton acquired the property from private owners with the help of a state grant. The land was considered undevelopable due to the wetlands, so the owners sold it to be preserved as a park.

The park, especially the dune area, is the natural habitat for many endangered species; such as the piping plover, which is a sparrow-sized bird that is most often seen running in and out of the surf seizing food much in the manner of the sandpiper; the least tern, which is a robin-sized bird that feeds by diving for fish; and the tiger beetle. Due to these and other endangered species, the preserve is monitored by the Department of Game and Inland Fisheries. April through September is considered the nesting season. Please stay on the beach and enjoy the view of the surroundings from that vantage point. Do not walk into the dune or marsh areas. This is a protected area and you may disturb nesting birds and other aspects of the natural environment.

Walk

The walk starts at the entrance to the park on State Park Drive and extends (depending on the tide) to Factory Point. The length of the beach out to Factory Point is 2 ½ miles one way. If you're not up to the full five miles round trip, walk as far as you want and turn around.

To begin the walk, enter the park through the vehicle barrier. Walk along the park service road, past a beautiful view of Hawkins Pond on your right, to the beach front. Turn left onto the beach and head toward Factory Point. Shortly after beginning the beach portion of the walk, you will notice a pile of rocks in the water near the shore. This is what is left of Lighthouse Point. As you walk along the beach, be sure to stay off the dunes as you will disturb the natural habitat if you venture off the beach. Factory Point is the turnaround point for the walk.

Points of Interest

1. **Lighthouse Point:** The Back River Lighthouse used to stand at the point shortly into the walk where you can see the remains (a pile of rocks) in the water. Three contractors originally bid on the contract to build Back River Lighthouse. Winslow Lewis, an inventor and supplier of lamps and reflectors, won the bid even though he had never built a lighthouse on the Chesapeake. Unfortunately, Mr. Lewis was unfamiliar with the area and miscalculated the projected location for the lighthouse. He assumed that it was to be constructed three miles farther north of the designated location. When he discovered the error, he had to make arrangements to move the supplies to the location by smaller boat since the water was too shallow for the original boat.

   Mr. William Jett became the first keeper of the light in 1829. He continued in the job until 1852 and lived in a house 144 feet inland. In 1903, a storm nearly destroyed the light keeper's house and the footbridge, but with 72 hours of repairs, both were saved. The light in Back River Lighthouse was automated in 1915, but in 1936, it stopped working and was never repaired. A hurricane destroyed the light keeper's house and the lighthouse in 1956. Eventually, both structures fell down, and all that remains is the pile of rocks you see at Lighthouse Point.

2. **Factory Point (Northend Point):** From Factory Point, you can easily see Plum Island Wildlife Refuge (managed by the US Department of the Interior) across the water in Poquoson. To the left of Factory Point is Back River where it extends into the salt marsh. To the right is the Chesapeake Bay.

Chapter 6:
New Kent

Warreneye

Warreneye Nature Trail

Key

Walks

P Parking

⭐ Start Here

- - - Trail

—— Loop

1) Old Road/Old Stage Road
2) Loblolly Pine Forest
3) Old Mines
4) Timber Harvest
5) Warreneye Church Site
6) Courtney Seed Orchard

Trail	Miles	Markers
Main Trail	2.5	Yellow
Fern Loop	0.2	Red
Marl Loop	0.4	White
Poplar Loop	0.3	Blue

Warreneye Nature Trail

Description

The Main Trail of the Warreneye Nature Trail is a beautiful wooded 2 ½ mile walk over very hilly terrain. This is more than a nature trail. The Chesapeake Forest Products Company owns the land and developed it, in part, to educate the public on man's use of the forest. The designers of this trail have succeeded in not only developing a picturesque setting for a pleasurable walk, but in devising an exceptional educational experience that can be enjoyed by the whole family. From gently flowing woodland streams and an example of the life cycle of a loblolly pine forest to the site of the Warreneye Church and the open fields of the Courtney Seed Orchard, the Warreneye Nature Trail offers one interesting site after another. Warreneye offers shorter versions of the 2 ½ mile walk by way of three loops that lead back to the trail entrance.

To enhance the walk, there is an excellent guidebook available at the entrance to the trail. Be sure to take one with you on the walk. The guidebook provides comprehensive explanations of numerous sites along the trail. Watch for the markers; and, to get the most from the walk, take time at each marker to read the corresponding passage. The guidebook blends background information about the many ways that man uses the forest with general nature information and history of the area. The Chesapeake Forest Products Company recommends that you call ahead if you will be taking 12 or more people on the walk to ensure that there are enough guidebooks available for the group.

Location

Warreneye Nature Trail is located in New Kent County. To reach the trail from I-64, take the West Point - Rt. 33 exit. Drive 3.8 miles toward West Point and turn right into the parking area at the trail entrance.

Parking and Facilities

There is plenty of parking at the trail entrance off Rt. 33. The only restroom is a Porta-Potty on the back side of the trail at the edge of Courtney Seed Orchard. The trail is open from sunrise to sunset. It is considered trespassing to be in Warreneye at other times.

Background

The paper mill has been the major industry of West Point since 1914. The Chesapeake Forest Products Company was first called The Chesapeake Pulp and Paper Company. It was located in West Point due to the natural resources of the area and West Point's proximity to the Pamunkey River and the railroad lines.

The paper products industry dates back nearly two hundred years prior to the establishment of the mill in West Point. Virginia has always been a major location of this industry. In 1744, the first mill of the South was built on a creek near Williamsburg when Benjamin Franklin financed William Parks, a Virginia printer, to make paper. Back then, paper was made by pulping soft rags. After 1850, technology advanced, and the industry converted from using rags to using tree pulp to make paper products. The mill at West Point was one of the first of its kind in North America.

Warreneye Nature Trail was developed in 1973 by the Chesapeake Forest Products Company to express their proactive approach to the public interest in promoting the best use of the land. The Chesapeake Forest Products Company purchased the bulk of the land in New Kent in 1926 and 1936. In 1971, the company began planning for the Warreneye Nature Trail. This planning concentrated on devising a trail that would highlight information on forest, soil and water management; wildlife; wild flowers; and local history.

In 1972, the company purchased 7 acres around the site of the Warreneye Church for the trail. They completed construction in 1973 and succeeded in providing a beautiful recreation spot for the residents of New Kent County and for visitors from around the country. It's easy to see why approximately 300 to 400 people use the trail yearly. The trail is frequented by hikers, joggers, bird watchers, boy scouts, girl scouts as well as members of the Virginia Native Plant Society. Representatives from the Smithsonian Institute heard of the trail and sent a research team to review it. After that visit, they commended Warreneye for the diversity of the ferns growing in the woods.

In addition to Warreneye Nature Trail, the Chesapeake Forest Products Company built another trail in Lancaster County. That one is called Corrotoman River Nature Trail. In their continuing campaign to provide interesting outdoor experiences to the general public, the Chesapeake Forest Products Company is considering developing more trails. Ideas under consideration include a trail for children and one that can be accessed by car, so that it can be enjoyed by people who may not be able to take advantage of hiking trails.

Walk

The walk begins at the entrance in the parking area. Just after the entrance to the walk, bear right onto the Main Trail. The Main Trail is well-marked with yellow paint on the trees. If you choose a shorter version of the walk, follow the Main Trail to one of the loops that leads through the woods to the backside of the Main Trail. The loops are marked as follows:

Fern Loop = red markings
Marl Loop = white markings
Poplar Loop = blue markings

There are several benches during the walk to relax and enjoy the scenery. Just watch for the trail markings on the trees, and you'll have no difficulty following the trail.

Points of Interest

Pick up the Warreneye Nature Trail guidebook at the trail entrance for a comprehensive list of over thirty points of interest on the walk. Here, we have highlighted a few of our favorites.

1. ***Old Road and Old Stage Road:*** This is a pre-Revolutionary road system that connected New Kent Courthouse and Williamsburg to Plum Point. The roadbed is visibly lower than the banks due to erosion caused by weather and use of the roads.

2. *Loblolly Pine Forest:* The paper industry relies heavily on the loblolly pine for pulp. Therefore, it is very important that the sites for loblolly pines are managed properly so that trees will flourish and when harvested are replaced. The loblolly pine forest at Station 6 shows an example of the care that is taken in maintaining this important resource.

3. *Old Mines:* Local farmers in the 1920s and 1930s mined the hills for marl and extracted the lime from it to put on their fields. You can see spots where they mined on the Main Trail and on the Marl Loop.

4. *Timber Harvest:* Once timber is harvested, the area must be protected to allow it to regenerate naturally. This is an example of a recently harvested area that is in the process of regeneration.

5. *Warreneye Church Site:* Warreneye Church was built in 1703. It was one of two pre-Revolutionary churches of the Blisland Parish. Although Warreneye Church was razed in the early 1800s, the other church, Hickory Neck, is still standing in Toano on Route 60. George Washington is said to have visited Warreneye Church twice while visiting his wife's sister at Basset mansion in Eltham.

6. *Courtney Seed Orchard:* The Chesapeake Forest Products Company uses the Courtney Seed Orchard to produce genetically improved pine seed. They use the seeds from the trees in the orchard to reforest other areas.

Footsteps: _____

Newport News Park

Mariners' Museum Park

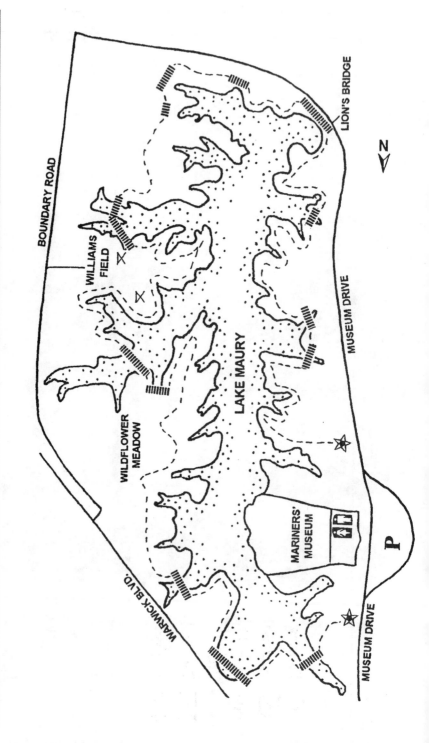

Key

P   Parking

  Restrooms

★   Start Here

– – –   Trail

✕   Picnic Area

||||| Bridge

Mariners' Museum Park

Description

The Noland Trail, which circles picturesque Lake Maury, is a 5 mile woodland, dirt trail with wooden bridges and scenic overlooks. The trail is laid out to capitalize on and preserve the natural beauty of Mariners' Museum Park and the lake. The bridges and four well-placed overlooks provide resting points to savor the view. Wildlife, such as waterfowl, birds, turtles, and fish can be observed in their natural habitat. A variety of trees, bushes, and wild flowers bloom seasonally. The trail provides variety during any season.

Location

The Noland Trail is located at Mariners' Museum Park in Newport News. To reach Mariners' Museum Park from I-64, take the J. Clyde Morris Blvd. exit toward Newport News. Follow J. Clyde Morris Blvd. for approximately 2 ½ miles. The park is at the end of J. Clyde Morris where it intersects with Warwick Blvd. Go straight across the intersection and into Mariners' Museum Park and follow the signs to the parking area in front of the museum.

Parking and Facilities

There is ample free parking in front of the museum. In case it's a busy day, there is an overflow lot for the Noland Trail just before you reach the museum. Restrooms are available at the museum as well as at the Williams Field Picnic Area. The trail is open daily from dawn to dusk.

Background

In the 1920s, Archer M. Huntington, scholar and philanthropist, and Anna Hyatt Huntington, sculptor, decided to build a museum dedicated to the culture of the sea. Their idea went beyond the museum, however. They set out to create a park as a backdrop for sculpture and to preserve the natural environment of the area. In

1930, they began to obtain the land for the park. By 1933, they had acquired 550 acres. In 1931, a dam (commonly known as Lion's Bridge) was built, creating Lake Maury which is 167 acres. The lake was named for Matthew Fontaine Maury who was a native Virginian and well-known oceanographer.

The Mariners' Museum is the only international maritime museum in the United States and is one of the largest in the world. It contains over 35,000 artifacts from maritime paintings and figureheads to ship models. There is also a research library that houses books, manuscripts, maps, and charts that preserve maritime history. One of the major objectives of the museum is education. The museum educational program provides workshops for school groups as well as community groups.

The Noland Trail, which is a complete 5 mile circuit around Lake Maury, was completed in 1991. Original trails date back to the 1930s when Mariners' Museum was built, but, at that time, the trails did not meet to circle the lake. Those early trails were originally bridle paths and were used by the patrons of a nearby stable. Later, after the stables closed, people continued to walk the trails. In 1985, Lloyd Noland, Jr. proposed connecting the walking trails around Lake Maury to make a continuous walking system circling the lake.

Walk

The Noland Trail is five miles in length. There are entrances to it on either side of Mariners' Museum. The route circles Lake Maury by way of a well-marked trail connected by 14 primary bridges. If you're not up to a 5 mile walk, you can choose either entrance and walk a portion of the trail then double back. Generally, the trail is less hilly if you take the entrance to the left of the museum (as you face the museum). You'll find picturesque views from the bridges and from any one of the four overlooks on the trail. Turtles are abundant in the lake and a variety of waterfowl can be seen on the water.

Points of Interest

1. *Lion's Bridge:* Two large stone lions adorn the bridge. It is the

dam that created Lake Maury in 1931 and provides a beautiful view of the James River.

2. *Mariners' Museum:* The museum is open daily from 10:00 a.m. to 5:00 p.m. except on Christmas. It exhibits over 35,000 artifacts of sea culture. Woodcrafters demonstrate their craft and historical interpreters tell of the lore of the sea at the museum.

3. *Mariners' Museum Park Library:* The library contains 75,000 volumes of books that date back to the early 1500s, covering ship and boat building, maritime history, and arts and technology related to the sea. In addition, the library contains approximately 5,000 maps relating to the Chesapeake Bay, 350,000 photographs, one million manuscript items (including the hull records from 1922 to 1980 of Chris-Craft Industries), 10,000 ship and boat plans, and ships' registers. It is open Monday through Saturday from 9:00 a.m. to 5:00 p.m.

4. *Gift Gallery:* This is the museum's gift shop and is next door to the museum. It contains a nice selection of books and gifts related to the sea.

5. *Picnic Area:* There are two picnic areas on the trail. One is located near Williams Field and can also be reached by car by way of a small road off Boundary Road. The other is on the trail about a quarter of a mile before Williams Field.

Newport News Park

FORT EUSTIS BLVD.

4

WHITE OAK

WYNN'S MILL

SWAMP FIRE

5

WHITE OAK

HORSE/BIKE TRAIL

.7 mi.

6

1.3 mi.

SYCAMORE CREEK

TWIN FORKS

LONG MEADOW

DAM #1

LEE HALL RESERVOIR

9

P 3

P

P

P?

HORSE/BIKE TRAIL

.5 mi.

8

7 - .4 mi.

JEFFERSON AVE.

N

Key

?	Park Hqtrs./Information
P	Parking
🚹🚺	Restrooms
▬	Park Road
- - -	Trail
✗	Picnic Area
‖‖‖	Bridge

1)	Boat Rentals/Fishing Area
2)	Ranger Station
3)	Interpretive Center
4)	Deer Run Golf Course
5)	Beaver Dam/Lodge
6)	George Washington's Hqtrs.
7)	Ropes and Initiative Course
8)	Archery Range
9)	Camping

Trail	Miles
White Oak	2.6
Wynn's Mill	1.2
Sycamore Creek	0.5
Twin Forks	0.7
Long Meadow	0.5
Swamp Fire	0.3
Horse/Bike	5.3

Description

Newport News Park trails offer an opportunity to get close to nature. On the walks, you'll see a variety of wildlife and environments. Deer are plentiful throughout the park, and there are beaver, river otter, gray and red foxes, racoons, rabbits, and striped skunks in addition to a wide variety of permanent and migratory birds. In all, there are approximately 200 species of birds and 30 species of mammals in the park. The Lee Hall Reservoir provides a stunning backdrop to this park. In addition, there are swamps, lakes, ponds, and streams to add variety.

For walking enthusiasts, there are approximately 15 miles of trails to explore, ranging from ½ mile in length to 5.3 miles. The most popular trail, White Oak Nature Trail, is 2.6 miles long. You can combine any of the trails. Many of them link together.

There's something for everyone within the 8,065 acre park. From camping to paddle boating and archery, Newport News Park has it all. Special programs and activities are offered throughout the year. History buffs will enjoy seeing the site of the Battle of Dam No. 1 and the earthen works and fortifications which are remnants of the Civil War. The Interpretive Center displays historic and nature exhibits and also is the Wildlife Rehabilitation Center, where they care for injured animals. The Interpretive Center is a good starting point for your visit to the park. Other attractions include a horse/bike trail, a Ropes and Initiatives Course, boat rentals, and an archery range. Newport News Park offers plenty of room for camping and has picnic and playground areas to enjoy.

Location

From Interstate 64, take the Fort Eustis exit (Rt. 105). Turn left onto Jefferson Avenue (Rt. 143) then turn right into the park entrance.

Parking and Facilities

Parking is available at the Park Headquarters near the entrance to the park and at the Interpretive Center. For easy access to the walking trails, it is best to park at the Interpretive Center. Restrooms are available at the Park Headquarters, the Interpretive Center, the Ranger Station, and in picnic area 3. In addition to walking, other activities include camping, paddle boating, biking, horse trail, archery, boat rentals, picnic areas, and playgrounds.

Background

Civil War earthworks and fortifications remind visitors that long ago this area was of historical significance and less peaceful than it is today. Dam No. 1 is the site of the 1862 battle between Confederate and Union soldiers. It is covered by water but can be seen from the bridge.

In 1862, the capital of the Confederacy was located in Richmond. President Lincoln was worried about protecting Washington, D.C. with the Confederates nearby. Therefore, Lincoln assigned Major General George B. McClellan to march on Richmond and take the capital away from the Confederates.

McClellan decided to approach Richmond from the south rather than marching on it from Washington, D.C. Therefore, he landed his troops at Fort Monroe at the southern end of the peninsula between the James River and the York River. On April 2, 1862, McClellan began his attempt to secure the area and move toward Richmond. Due to faulty maps and poor information, McClellan had a more difficult time than he expected. He never made it to Richmond. Instead, he eventually diverted to Yorktown and then to Washington. He did move his troops partway up the peninsula, however, and the area that is now Newport News Park saw one of the battles of the Civil War.

On April 16, 1862, Union soldiers marched through the water, attacked the Confederate soldiers just below Dam No. 1 and captured the earthworks along the edge of the water. The Confederates fell back. The Union soldiers only held their position for a short while because they had no reinforcements backing them and their ammunition was waterlogged from crossing the water. There was a second attack that same day, but little progress was made as the fighting was called off at nightfall. Today, visitors can see ten miles of Civil War fortifications and earthworks along the walking trails in Newport News Park, and the Interpretive Center contains artifacts from this historical time.

The city of Newport News made a wise decision in preserving this area for a park. It has designed a recreational haven for the entire community and the many tourists who visit here. The park is one of the largest municipal parks in the United States.

Walks

1. ***White Oak Trail (2.6 miles):*** The White Oak Trail is a loop with interpretive markers that correspond with the nature points of interest described in a booklet available in the Interpretive Center. On this walk, you'll see a beaver lodge near the swamp bridge.

2. ***Wynn's Mill Trail (1.2 miles):*** The Wynn's Mill Trail starts toward the far end of White Oak Trail. Therefore, mileage for this walk must be combined with that of White Oak Trail. You'll see earthworks on this trail.

3. ***Sycamore Creek Trail (.5 miles):*** The Sycamore Creek Trail connects the White Oak Trail and the Horse/Bike Trail.

4. ***Twin Forks Trail (.7 miles):*** The Twin Forks Trail can be easily combined with the Long Meadow Trail (.5 miles one way) to make a 1.7 mile walk. Twin Forks Trail has position markings for the Battle of Dam No. 1.

5. ***Long Meadow Trail (.5 miles):*** The Long Meadow Trail extends from the Lee Hall Resevoir to the Horse/Bike Trail.

6. ***Swamp Fire Trail (.3 miles):*** The Swamp Fire Trail connects Wynn's Mill Trail with the Horse/Bike Trail.

7. ***Horse/Bike Trail (5.3 miles):*** The Horse/Bike Trail starts at the Park Headquarters. Halfway through the trail is a short walk to the site of George Washington's Headquarters in the Colo-

nial National Historic Park. There are trails of .7 miles, 1.3 miles, and .5 miles that cut across from one side of the Horse/Bike Trail to the other for a shorter walk. These shortcuts are marked on the map.

Points of Interest:

1. *Boating:* Newport News Park has over 650 acres of water fully stocked with fish. There are paddle boats, canoes and Jon boats for rent. There are also two boat ramps for small boats.

2. *Ranger Station:* General information about the park and the many activities, facilities and programs offered by the park are available at the Ranger Station.

3. *Interpretive Center:* The Interpretive Center contains interesting historic and nature exhibits. In addition, it is the Wildlife Rehabilitation Center. From the footbridge near the Interpretive Center, you can see the remnants of Dam No. 1. Dam No. 1 is about midway on the 12 mile defense line Major General John Bankhead Magruder (Confederate) established between Mulberry Island (now Fort Eustis) toward Yorktown.

4. *Deer Run Golf Course.*

5. *Beaver Dam/Lodge:* On White Oak Trail, you'll see the work of beavers.

6. *George Washington's Headquarters:* The site of George Washington's headquarters during the Revolutionary War is a short walk from the middle of the Horse/Bike Trail. It is located on the adjacent land of the Colonial National Historic Park.

7. *Ropes and Initiates Course:* This is just one of the many programs offered by the park.

8. *Archery Range:* The park has three field archery ranges and a practice range. You must provide your own equipment, but targets are provided.

9. *Camping:* 189 campsites are located near the Park Headquarters. Camping facilities are complete with restrooms and showers, laundry room, camp store and playground equipment. There are handicapped accessible sites as well.

Chapter 8:
Norfolk

Hunter House

Ghent-Chrysler Museum

REDGATE AVE.

RALEIGH AVE.

BOISSEVAIN AVE.

STOCKLEY GARDENS

DUNDAFF ST.

BLOW ST.

REDGATE AVE.

RALEIGH AVE.

BOISSEVAIN AVE.

OLNEY RD.

MOWBRAY ARCH

COLONIAL AVE.

FAIRFAX AVE.

PEMBROKE AVE.

WARREN CRES.

MILL ST.

COLONIAL AVE.

DRUMMOND PL.

MOWBRAY

BOTETOURT ST.

ARCH

OLNEY RD.

MEMORIAL PL.

GRACE ST.

DUKE ST.

BRAMBLETON AVE.

BOUSH ST.

YARMOUTH

MOWBRAY ARCH S

SMITH

CREEK

N

Key

P Parking

🚹🚺 Restrooms

⭐ Start Here

- - - Walk

1) Chrysler Museum
2) Holland House
3) Christ and St. Luke's Episcopal Church

Description

The Ghent District of Norfolk is one of the oldest and most beautiful areas of the city. Some aspects of this area resemble Greenwich Village in New York City. Spacious residences converted to apartments for artists and students sit side-by-side with some of the most beautiful older homes of Norfolk. The walk through this area starts at the Chrysler Museum. Allow enough time before or after the walk to wander through the exhibits of the museum. The Wall Street Journal has rated the collection at the Chrysler Museum as one of the top 20 collections in the country. The museum contains a world-renowned glass collection, a collection of European paintings as well as an American collection, a decorative arts collection, sculpture, and photography. It contains artwork from 2700 BC to the present.

The walk is 2 miles in length and winds along the Hague, part of the Smith Creek Inlet of the Elizabeth River, the Stockley Garden neighborhood and back. You'll pass many Victorian style homes along the way and see the picturesque Christ and St. Luke's Church.

Location

To reach the Chrysler Museum from I-64, take Rt. 264 toward Norfolk. From 264, take the Waterside Drive exit and follow Waterside until it becomes Bousch Street. Follow Bousch Street through several traffic lights, including the one at Brambleton Avenue to Olney Road. Turn left onto Olney Road. Chrysler Museum is at the next intersection on the corner of Olney Road and Duke Street.

Parking and Facilities

If you're intending to visit Chrysler Museum, park in the museum parking lot. If you are going to skip the museum, there is parallel parking available on Mowbray Arch behind the museum. Restrooms are available at the museum.

Safety Tip
This is a city walk, so keep children close and watch carefully when crossing the streets.

Background
The neighborhood known as the Ghent Historic District was originally designed by John Graham from Philadelphia. Between 1890 and 1905, this area took shape with middle class and upper class homes designed in Victorian, Queen Anne and Colonial Revival styles.

Ghent has been compared to Greenwich Village of New York City because it is home to a diverse group of people. Writers, artists, and students live next to lawyers, doctors and executives, and the neighborhoods are peppered with original homes, apartment buildings, cafes, and boutiques.

The original Ghent dates back to a farm called Pleasant Point. In 1814, the farm was re-named Ghent after the Treaty of Ghent. The treaty resulted in the opening of the port of Norfolk after the War of 1812. The farm remained through 1890.

Adolph Boissevain, a Dutchman, financed the development of Ghent as a subdivision of Norfolk after the Civil War. The area of the walk was designed along the Y-shaped Smith Creek with semi-circular streets that afford a scenic view of the water. Most of the original buildings still stand in this planned suburb designed as a contrast to the more densely populated areas of Norfolk.

Walk
The walk starts behind the Chrysler Museum on Grace Street. Walk along Grace Street to Memorial and turn right. Walk to Mowbray Arch and turn left. Cross Mowbray Arch at Drummond. Take Drummond to Warren Crescent and turn left. Continue on Warren Crescent to Pembroke and turn left. Go to Mowbray Arch and turn right. Follow Mowbray Arch to Olney road. Cross Olney to Christ and St. Luke's Catholic Church. Walk to the left side of the church and turn right onto Stockley Gardens. Walk to Redgate and

turn left. Cross to the other side of Stockley Gardens and turn left and walk back to Olney Road. When you reach Olney again, walk to Mowbray Arch and turn right. Return to where you parked.

Points of Interest

1. ***Chrysler Museum:*** The Chrysler Museum houses 30,000 objects of art, featuring items representative of nearly 4,000 years. The Jean Outland Chrysler Library is also maintained within the Chrysler Museum. It contains more than 40,000 volumes on art as well as videotapes, sales catalogues as far back as the 18th century, and monographs of major artists. The museum was founded in 1933 and was first called the Norfolk Museum of Arts and Sciences. In 1971, it was renamed the Chrysler Museum to honor Walter P. Chrysler, Jr. who donated approximately half of the current collection of art. The museum also contains Pallate's Cafe where you can take a break for brunch or lunch.

2. ***Holland House:*** The Holland House Apartment Building on the corner of Drummond and Mowbray Arch is listed as a Virginia National Historic Landmark. It was built as a hotel for the Jamestown Exposition of 1907. Holland House was designed by a Dutch architect with a large dining room, a kitchen, barber shop, and store on the first floor. The restaurant became a popular lunch spot of Ghent during the 1930s to 1950s. Holland House was renovated in 1983 and today is used as an apartment building.

3. ***Christ and St. Luke's Episcopal Church:*** The first church of the Elizabeth River Parish was erected in 1637. Christ and St. Luke's Episcopal Church was part of that parish and was built in 1909 and 1910 across Olney Road from Smith Creek. Watson Huckle of Philadelphia designed it in the Late Gothic Revival style. The picturesque site of the church is rivaled by the beauty of the interior with its many wooden carvings, detailed windows and tower.

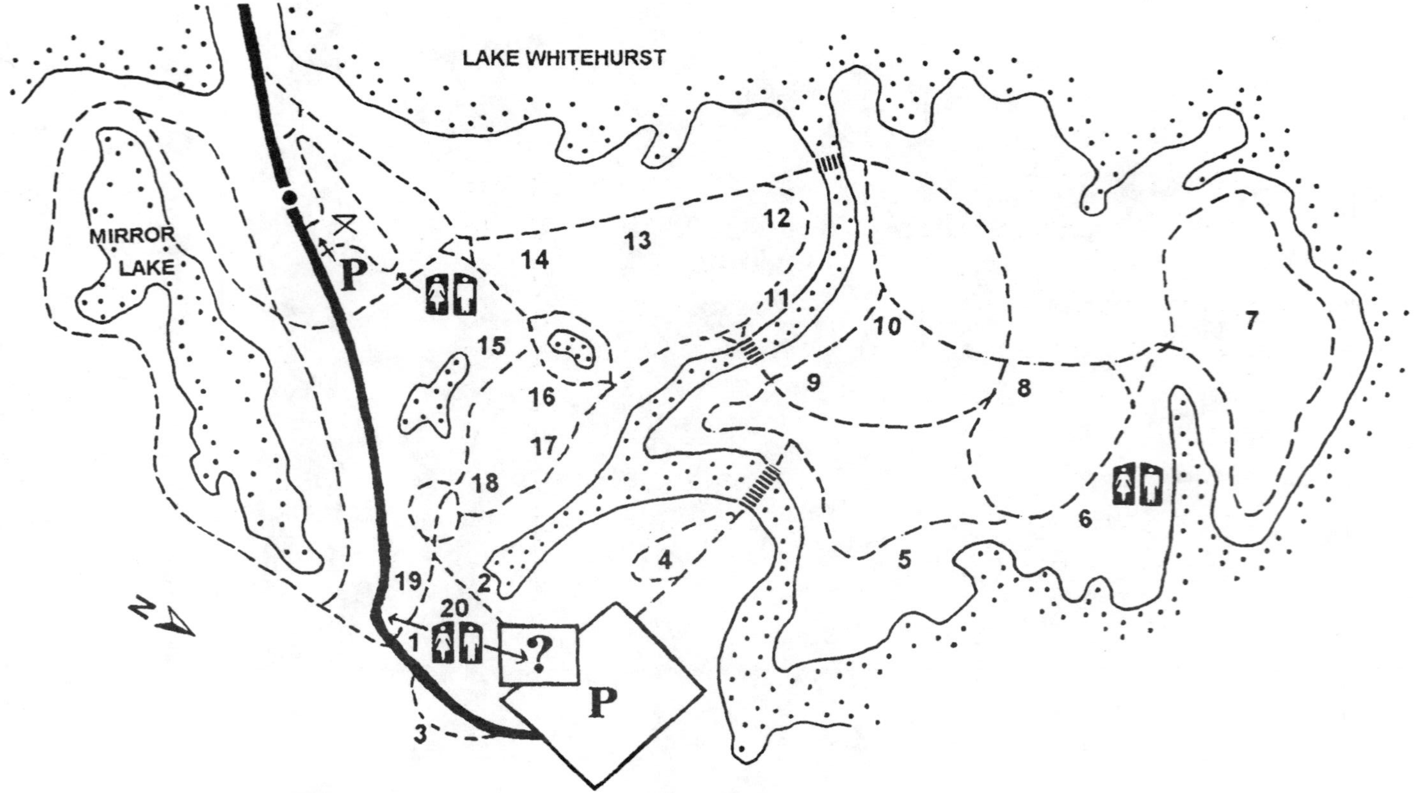

Norfolk Botanical Garden

LAKE WHITEHURST

MIRROR LAKE

7

6

8

5

10

9

12

11

4

13

14

15

16

17

18

19

20

2

3

1

P

P

P

?

N

Key

- Contact Station
? Visitor Center
P Parking
🚹🚺 Restrooms
▬ Garden Road
- - - Path
✗ Picnic Area
▦ Bridge

1) Cafe
2) Boat/Train Tour
3) Airport Overlook
4) Rose Garden
5) Nature Trail
6) Wildflower Meadow
7) Enchanted Forest
8) Flowering Aboretum
9) All American Garden
10) Baker Overlook

11) Colonial Garden
12) Healing Garden
13) Statuary Vista
14) Rhododendron Collection
15) Camellia Garden
16) Renaissance Garden
17) English Border Garden
18) Holly Garden
19) Perennial Garden
20) Japanese Garden
Tropical Pavilion

Norfolk Botanical Garden

Description

Walking through the Norfolk Botanical Garden is much more than a nature walk. It is a celebration of horticulture at its best. As you walk along any of the 12 miles of paths, you'll wind past one carefully designed garden after another. No matter what season you choose to visit the garden, you'll find something in bloom. Because Lake Whitehurst virtually borders the garden, waterfowl can be seen here in abundance. They rest and feed on the lake, and there is a duck feeding area near the entrance to the garden. A canal from Lake Whitehurst winds through the garden. There are interpretive boat tours through the park for a way to see the lush scenery from a different vantage point. Mirror Lake borders another side.

Visitors to Norfolk Botanical Garden are delighted and impressed by the care that has been taken in designing this beautiful, peaceful setting. Benches throughout the garden invite you to relax and take in the scenery. In spring, 200,000 azaleas turn the garden into a fairyland of shades of pink, rose, mauve, and white. In addition to the azaleas, camellias and dogwood color the entire garden, and specific areas have been planted to highlight individual species. Roses and tulips occupy their own areas, and there is a Japanese Garden, Perennial Garden, Colonial Herb Garden and Wildflower Meadow to name a few of the many attractions. The Tropical Pavilion is 3,600 square feet and houses 100 species of plants and rain forest foliage.

Location

Norfolk Botanical Garden is located in Norfolk adjacent to Norfolk International Airport. From I-64, take the Norview Avenue East exit toward the airport. Turn left onto Azalea Garden Road then right into the garden at the entrance. There is an admission fee at the contact station.

Parking and Facilities

From the contact station, follow the road to the parking area at the end of the road. Restrooms are available at the Visitor Center and at various locations in the garden. Picnic facilities are located near the Contact Station. There is a gift shop in the Visitor Center and a Garden Teahouse in Norfolk Botanical Garden.

Background

In 1938, the Garden started with the planting of 4,000 azaleas. The Norfolk Botanical Garden encompasses 155 acres between Lake Whitehurst and the Norfolk International Airport. Over the years, planting continued with azaleas eventually adding up to 200,000. They also added 700 varieties of camellias and 250 varieties of rhododendron.

After 1958 when phase two was started, thousands of varieties of plants were added to create diversity and to make the horticulture collection within the Garden one of the finest on the east coast. In 1962, the Japanese Garden was built and in 1955 it was redesigned to add hills, a waterfall and reflecting pool. The Japanese Garden was built to honor Kitakyushu, Japan, which is Norfolk's sister city.

Also in 1962 and 1963, the majority of the statues in the Statuary Vista were donated by Bruce Dunstan and Vincent Speranza of Richmond, Virginia. There are eleven statues in all. They were originally carved by Moses Ezekiel in Rome between 1879 and 1884 for the Corona Gallery in Washington, D.C. As you walk down the Statuary Vista, you'll walk past statues of the artists Rembrandt, daVinci, Rubens and Durer.

In 1963, the Fragrance Garden for the blind was financed by the City of Norfolk and the Tidewater District of the Virginia Federation of Garden Clubs.

During the bicentennial in 1976, the Rose Garden was dedicated to celebrate the nation's 200th birthday. The rose, often proclaimed "queen of the flowers," is grown for its fragrance and beauty. The 4,000 rose bushes produce over 250,000 roses a year. They bloom in the summer, adding brilliant colors and fragrance to the garden.

Footsteps: _____

In 1984, the Garden created the Renaissance Garden. Yearly, the Azalea Queen of the International Azalea Festival, which is a festival in honor of the North Atlantic Treaty Organization, is crowned in this area. It has a wide vista with stone fences and grassy terraces. The four statues on the upper terrace depict the four seasons. The beauty of the Renaissance Garden is completed by a fountain and reflecting pool.

In addition to these larger gardens, there are many smaller collections that delight visitors of Norfolk Botanical Garden. To enhance the visit for everyone, there are also interpretive boat tours and trackless train tours for an additional fee. Weddings, outdoor concerts, plant sales, and educational programs take place within the garden throughout the year.

Walk

There are 12 miles of paths throughout the Garden. This is the perfect spot to devise your own walk depending on how far you want to go. Start at the Visitor Center where interpretative materials are available.

Norfolk Historic Freemason Walk

ATLANTIC ST.

P

1

2

MARTIN'S LANE

WATERSIDE DR.

FREEMASON ST.

COLLEGE PL.

TAZEWELL ST.

BROCHE AVE.

CITY HALL AVE.

PLUME ST.

MAIN ST.

BOUSCH ST.

BOUSCH ST.

8

4

5

3

7

9

6

17

DUKE ST.

BROCHE AVE.

COLLEGE PL.

TAZEWELL ST.

11

10

15

12

YARMOUTH ST.

13

COLLEGE CROSS

DUNMORE ST.

W. FREEMASON ST.

BOTETOURT ST.

14

16

ELIZABETH RIVER

N

Key

P Parking

🚹🚺 Restrooms

⭐ Start Here

- - - Walk

‖‖‖‖ Bridge/Walkway

1) The Waterside Parking Garage
2) The Waterside
3) Town Point Park
4) Customs House
5) World Trade Center
6) Nauticus
7) Freemason Abbey
8) Epworth United Methodist Church
9) Taylor Whittle House

10) Hunter House Victorian Museum
11) Glisson House
12) Judge Thomas H. Wilcox House
13) Petty-Dixon House
14) Selden House
15) Allmand-Archer House
16) Marine Observation Tower
17) Mainmast

Footsteps: ————————————————————
Norfolk Historic Freemason Walk

Description

Norfolk is an historic seaport city on the Elizabeth River's Eastern Branch. The history of Norfolk began only a little more than 70 years after the first colonists established the settlement at Jamestown. In 1680, King Charles II of England commanded that each Virginia county purchase 50 acres to be laid out as a town. For 10,000 pounds of tobacco, Nicholas Wise, Jr. purchased the land with boundaries where the Elizabeth River, Water Street and City Hall Avenue are now. In 1682, the deed was recorded for Norfolk Towne. Norfolk has played an important part thoughout history with its strategic location as a port town between Philadelphia and Charleston. The Norfolk Historic Freemason Walk blends a look at the revitalized harbor area with the history of one of Virginia's oldest cities. It starts at The Waterside festival marketplace and takes you through Town Point Park, a lovely harbor-front park, in front of Nauticus, then on to the historic Freemason residential neighborhood where you'll walk down a cobblestone road dotted with beautifully maintained original Norfolk homes. This is a walk that will appeal to boat lovers as well; you'll have a good view of the ships, sailboats, and yachts in the harbor throughout the walk.

Location

The Norfolk Historic Freemason Walk is located in downtown Norfolk. From I-64 take route 264 toward Norfolk. Exit at Waterside Drive and proceed to the Waterside parking garage on the right side of the street across from The Waterside.

Parking and Facilities

Parking is available in The Waterside parking garage. There is a fee for parking. Public restrooms, boutiques and restaurants are available in The Waterside.

Safety Tip

As this is a city walk be sure to stick to the route and to walk during daylight hours.

Background

King Charles II instructed Governor Culpeper in 1680 to develop towns in the Virginia Colony. To fulfill this directive, the Assembly allotted 50 acres for port towns in 20 counties. Norfolk, at the mouth of the Elizabeth River's Eastern Branch, was one of these. It was purchased in 1680 by Nicholas Wise, Jr. for 10,000 pounds of tobacco and deeded in 1682.

On October 17, 1683, Peter Smith, a sailor, bought the first three lots and became the first resident of Norfolk. The development of Norfolk got off to a slow start as Smith remained the only landowner for the next three years. In 1736, the King authorized Norfolk's charter. Samuel Bousch, a merchant, became the first mayor and Sir John Randolph was named to the position of recorder. In 1739, Borough Church (later re-named as St. Paul's Episcopal Church) was built.

Originally, Norfolk was all but an island surrounded by the Elizabeth River, Back Creek, and Newton Creek. Eventually, much of the creekbeds were filled in to provide easier access to the town. Norfolk became the docking point for many of the English ships as they were too large to reach plantation wharfs.

Norfolk's growth was thwarted several times throughout history. First, during the Revolutionary War, two thirds of Norfolk was destroyed when Lord Dunmore, the Royal Governor, bombarded it. Shortly thereafter, Colonial troops burned the rest of it to the ground to prevent Dunmore from using Norfolk for shelter. St. Paul's Episcopal Church survived the bombardment and still has a cannonball embedded in the east wall.

Norfolk bounced back from that destruction with the help of English and Scottish merchants who set up shops. Major fires in 1799 and 1804 slowed Norfolk's growth, and bouts of yellow fever in 1795, 1802, and 1804 took many lives and added to Norfolk's troubled progress. Next, the War of 1812 decreased Norfolk's exports drastically. Over the next couple of decades, Norfolk began to recover, and it became a city in 1845. The next setback came only two years later when a third of the population died of yellow fever.

Another slowdown to development came when the Civil War broke out. The city was occupied by Federal troops, under the command of General Benjamin F. "Beast" Butler, for a difficult nine years.

Growth and progress returned toward the end of the 19th century when Norfolk grew into the leading coal-exporting city. Norfolk's importance continued to grow during World War I and World War II due to its proximity to the water. The growth of the naval bases and the shipbuilding industry sustained Norfolk through both wars. During World War II, the influx of shipyard workers and sailors doubled Norfolk's population.

After World War II, Norfolk faced problems with numerous slums. The city set out in 1947 to solve its urban problems by winning the first urban renewal grant. They used it to clear approximately 1,000 acres of slums.

In the 1960s, Norfolk became the financial hub for the state when the region's banks established Norfolk as their headquarters. In recent years, the city has continued to grow and has capitalized on the tourist industry by razing the rundown harbor area and developing The Waterside festival marketplace, the World Trade Center, the Nauticus (with its 120,000 square feet devoted to maritime technology exhibits), and Harbor Park (the home of the Tidewater Tides baseball team). Norfolk takes pride in these new developments as well as maintaining the many historic structures.

Walk (2 miles)

Park at The Waterside parking garage. Exit the parking garage and cross Waterside Drive, toward The Waterside, at Martin's Lane. Turn right and walk past the Spirit of Norfolk yacht and up Waterside Drive toward Bousch Street on the street side of Town Point Park. After you round the curve across from the World Trade Center, Waterside Drive becomes Bousch Street. Walk past the front of The Nauticus. Continue on Bousch Street until you reach Freemason Street. Turn left onto Freemason Street. Continue to the end of

Freemason Street. Turn around and return along Freemason Street to the first corner and turn right onto Botetourt Street. Follow Botetourt Street and turn left onto College Place. Turn right onto College Cross and walk to the Marine Observation Tower. Follow the sidewalks toward Nauticus. In front of Nauticus, take the path along the harbor through Town Point Park. Turn left at the Mainmast and return to The Waterside and the parking garage.

Points of Interest

1. *The Waterside parking garage:* Start the walk here.

2. *The Waterside:* The Waterside was built in the mid-1980s. It was hoped that the addition of The Waterside festival market-place would revitalize the downtown area of Norfolk, and it has done just that. The Waterside has two levels. The upper level is packed with many boutiques and eight restaurants. The lower level contains a food court where many varieties of ethnic dishes are available. In the center of the lower level is a stage where entertainment adds to the festive atmosphere while you eat. Outside, toward the water, The Waterside is bordered by a wide, concrete boardwalk with benches where you can sit and enjoy a view of the busy harbor, or you can take a leisurely walk toward Town Point Park and get a closer look at the luxury yachts and sailboats moored at the dock. Ferry service is available to Portside across the harbor. Also, harbor cruises and trolley tours start at The Waterside.

3. *Town Point Park:* The Town Point Park area was built adjacent to the Waterside. It is home to countless music and art festivals throughout the year. When walking along the sidewalk near the water, you'll have a beautiful unobstructed view of the Elizabeth River. There are numerous benches throughout the park.

4. *Customs House:* The Customs House faces Main Street but backs onto Waterside Drive next to the World Trade Center. It's worth a trip to the front of it to see this Ammi B. Young building that was built between 1852 and 1860. Young was the supervising architect of the Treasury Department. He designed seventy customs houses and other government buildings during his

career. The building opened in 1858 and originally housed Customs and the Post Office. Today, it still houses Customs. This Historic Virginia Landmark served as a dungeon during the Federal occupation of Norfolk from 1862-1865.

5. **World Trade Center:** The World Trade Center rounds the corner of Waterside Drive and Bousch Street and houses numerous commercial businesses. With the revitalization of Norfolk, the addition of this business complex provided space for many businesses wanting to be in the heart of the business district.

6. **Nauticus:** The National Maritime Center is an interactive marine experience within a 120,000 square foot building. It offers 100 maritime exhibits from a 3-D underwater environment to drilling for oil offshore to petting a shark and taking part in a naval battle. The technology of virtual reality, a giant screen theater, and interactive videos set this museum apart from the usual. The exhibition of the power of the sea is a hit with children as well as adults. There is an admission fee.

7. **Freemason Abbey:** The Freemason Abbey was built in 1873. Originally, it was the home of the Second Presbyterian Church, then the Christian Scientists, and later the Odd Fellows. In 1989, it was renovated and converted to a restaurant. The restaurant has preserved the original stained glass. The Freemason Abbey is a beautiful spot for lunch or dinner.

8. **Epworth United Methodist Church:** The Epworth United Methodist Church was founded in 1850 and was located on the corner of Freemason Street and Granby Street. By 1890, the congregation had grown so large that the congregation decided to build a new church. The property on the corner of Freemason Street and Bousch Street was chosen as the new site. The cornerstone was laid in 1894 and the congregation named the church after the boyhood home of John Wesley. The church was constructed in the shape of a cross. The bell tower, 22 stained glass windows, interior Corinthian columns, and a stained glass dome in the center of the sanctuary enhance its beauty.

9. *Taylor Whittle House:* This Federal-style, brick town house was built in 1791 for Norfolk Mayor John Cowper. In 1803, he sold it to Richard Taylor, an importer. His son, Lt. Col. Walter Herron Taylor, who was on the staff of General Robert E. Lee, inherited the house. The house continued to be passed from generation to generation. Alexina Taylor, Walter Taylor's daughter, was the next occupant of the house. Her husband, Richard Page went with Commodore Perry to Japan. Elizabeth Page, Alexina and Richard Page's daughter, inherited the house next. She married William Conway Whittle. He was the executive officer on the CSS Shenandoah. In 1972, the house was willed to the Norfolk Historic Foundation. The foundation renovated the house.

10. *Hunter House Victorian Museum:* This house was built in 1894. This three story house is an excellent example of Richardsonian Romanesque architecture. It was designed by the Boston architect W.D. Wentworth. Today it is a Victorian museum. It contains the furnishings of James Wilson Hunter, including a nursery full of toys and Victorian furniture and the medical office of one of his sons, Dr. James Wilson Hunter, Jr., who was a physician. There is an herb garden in the back. There is an admission fee to tour the house.

11. *Glisson House:* Commodore Oliver S. Glisson built Glisson House around 1835. It is a three story brick house with a square cupola. Glisson House is an example of Greek Revival and Italianate style architecture.

12. *Judge Thomas H. Wilcox House:* This house was built around 1840. Today, it is an office building, but during World War II, it was used as a rooming house and called the Carolina Inn. The etched glass doors and windows add to its beauty.

13. *Petty-Dixon House:* The Petty-Dixon House was built in 1852 by William H. Addington. Four years later, Mrs. Hannah M. Petty bought it. Later, she sold it to William C. Dickson. The house has been used at different times as a residence and for commercial purposes.

14. **Selden House:** Dr. William Boswell Selden, Surgeon General of the Confederate Army, built this residence in 1807. It stands on a beautiful piece of land and the carriage houses extend to the water. The house was seized during the Civil War and served as headquarters for the Confederate army. In 1870, Dr. Selden played host to Robert E. Lee when he visited Norfolk.

15. **Allmand-Archer House:** The Allmand-Archer House is one of the oldest in Norfolk. It is another example of a Federal style town house. It was built in 1790 by a local merchant, Matthew Heary. He sold it to Harriston Allmand in 1802. The house passed to his sons then to his granddaughter, Elizabeth, who married William Archer. In 1974, the house was willed to the Norfolk Historical Society. The society sold it to John Richard and Louise Richard in 1977.

16. **Marine Observation Tower:** The observation tower occupies a beautiful spot on the river. It was constructed to commemorate the 1983 visit of Dr. Lee Teng Hui, the President of the Republic of China, then Governor of Taiwan Province. Virginia is their sister state.

17. **Mainmast:** This is the mainmast of the Schooner Atlantic, skippered by Charlie Barr in 1905. The schooner held the transatlantic speed record for 75 years. In World War I, it was used as a naval vessel. In World War II, the schooner was used by the Coast Guard for training.

Points of Interest in the Vicinity

1. **MacArthur Memorial:** Originally, the building housing the MacArthur Memorial was built as the city hall and courthouse for Norfolk. William Singleton designed the building. It was started in 1847 and completed in 1850. It served both purposes until 1918. It continued as the courthouse until 1960. Norfolk was the birthplace of General Douglas MacArthur's mother. Therefore, he chose Norfolk for his memorial and library. The interior of the building was redesigned by William and Geoffrey Platt with Finely Ferguson to house MacArthur's tomb and the many items representative of his distinguished military career.

2. *St. Paul's Episcopal Church:* This brick church was built in 1739 and, with its 30 inch thick walls, was the only structure left standing after Norfolk was bombarded by Lord Dunmore on January 1, 1776. A cannonball fired from the frigate Liverpool is still lodged in the east wall. Although it was still standing after the bombardment, St. Paul's Episcopal Church (then known as Borough Church) suffered damage and remained in disrepair for nine years. In 1786, a lottery raised the money to repair it. Due to disputes in the congregation, the church was abandoned in 1803. It was used for the next several years by various denominations. In 1832, it again became an Episcopal church. The church is built on 1.75 acres and is in the shape of a Latin Cross. A wall surrounds the grounds. The parish museum contains the chair John Hancock is said to have used to sign the Declaration of Independence.

Footsteps: _____

Chapter 9:
Virginia Beach

False Cape State Park

Back Bay National Wildlife Refuge

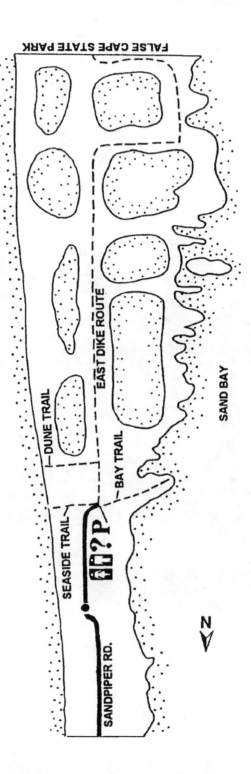

Key

- • Park Entrance
- ? Visitor Contact Station
- **P** Parking
- 🚹🚺 Restrooms
- - - - Trail
- ▬▬ Park Road

Walks

Trail	Miles
Bay	0.4
Seaside	0.25
Dune	0.5
East Dike	4.25

False Cape State Park

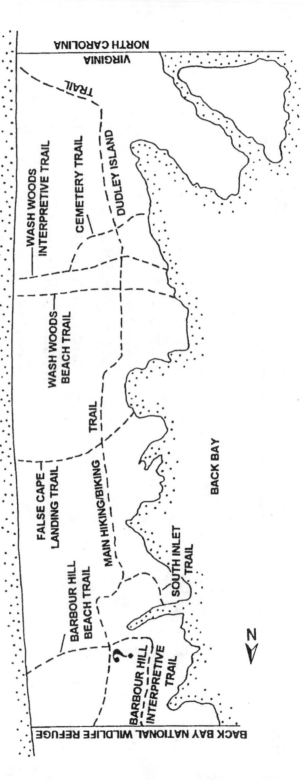

Key

? Contact Station/Information

- - - - Trail

Walks

Trail	Miles
Barbour Hill Interpretive	2.4
Barbour Hill Beach	0.7
South Inlet	0.4
False Cape Landing	0.6
Wash Woods Beach	0.8
Wash Woods Interpretive	0.7
Cemetery	0.5
Dudley Island	3.0
Main Hiking/Biking	4.3

Back Bay National Wildlife Refuge -- False Cape State Park

Description

Wildlife everywhere. The Back Bay National Wildlife Refuge covers 7,732 acres. If that isn't enough, you can take a 4.25 mile walk to reach False Cape State Park which encompasses another 4,321 acres. Both areas show off the beach, dune, woodland, and marsh habitats to their fullest. There is an abundance of wildlife to see, so bring your binoculars. You may spot osprey, wild ponies, Canada geese, snow swans, feral pigs, seagulls, ducks, songbirds, turtles, great blue heron, egret, white-tailed deer, rabbits, pelicans, and more. With at least 288 species of birds, this is a paradise for birders as well as nature enthusiasts.

The walks at Back Bay National Wildlife Refuge were designed to highlight the spectacular beauty of the refuge without disturbing the environment. From the Visitor Contact Station, you can follow several trails depending on what habitat you want to visit. Boardwalks across the dunes lead to the beach via the Seaside and Dune Trails. The marsh habitat is the most prevalent at Back Bay. It covers 75% of the refuge. For a good view of this habitat, take the Bay Trail. It is a straight, wide path with marsh on each side. Follow it to the end for a scenic view of Sand Bay. You will also see the marsh habitat along the East Dike route. If you walk the entire 4.25 miles of it, you'll reach False Cape State Park.

False Cape State Park is unique because it is undeveloped. There are only a few such areas on the east coast. The main hiking/biking trail cuts a path down the middle of False Cape State Park to Dudley Island Trail that leads to the southernmost portion of the park. The trails off the main hiking/biking trail vary in length from .4 miles to 2.4 miles. They showcase Back Bay and the ocean. The overlooks on the Barbour Hill Interpretive Trail and the South Inlet

Trail offer breathtaking views and excellent opportunities for photography.

The walking possibilities within Back Bay National Wildlife Refuge and False Cape State Park are endless. Regardless of the route you choose, you are guaranteed a memorable outdoor experience.

Location

To reach Back Bay National Wildlife Refuge from I-64, take the Rt. 44 East exit toward Virginia Beach. From Rt. 44 East, take the Birdneck Road exit. At the bottom of the exit, turn right onto Birdneck Road (from here, follow the signs to Sandbridge). Next, turn right onto General Booth Blvd., then turn left onto Princess Anne Road. Turn left onto Sandbridge Road (Rt. 269). In Sandbridge, turn right onto Sandpiper Road and follow the signs to the refuge which is at the end of the road. There is a fee to enter the refuge.

Parking and Facilities

Parking and restrooms are available at the Visitor Contact Station of Back Bay National Wildlife Refuge. Vehicles are not permitted in False Cape State Park and only pit toilets are available. False Cape State Park can only be reached by hiking, biking, or by boat. There is a Contact Station for the park on the main hiking/biking trail. To walk to the park, you can follow either the 4.25 mile East Dike route through Back Bay National Wildlife Refuge or walk the beach which is a little shorter. The refuge is open during daylight hours. All but the beach portion of the refuge is closed from November 1 through April 1. False Cape State Park is open year round during daylight hours. There are primitive campsites within the park. Reservations for camping are required. In addition, the Wash Woods Environmental Education Center is available by reservation for overnight educational groups. This facility is a renovated hunt club that sleeps 22.

Safety Tips

1. When visiting False Cape State Park, it's important to take precautions to avoid dehydration. It is recommended that you take a gallon of water per person with you if you walk to False Cape State Park because no drinkable water is available.

2. To protect the environment, be sure to stay on the designated trails.

3. There are poisonous snakes in these areas, so don't stray from the trails and stay alert.

4. No swimming is allowed on the beach.

5. Tics are prevalent in this area. Be sure to check for tics after your walk.

Background

Back Bay National Wildlife Refuge and False Cape State Park are two distinct areas on the map, with the Back Bay National Wildlife Refuge managed by the U.S. Fish and Wildlife Service and False Cape State Park managed by the Department of Conservation and Recreation of the Commonwealth of Virginia. The two blend together into a sanctuary for wildlife and waterfowl.

You will notice a distinct contrast between the two areas. Back Bay Wildlife Refuge is aggressively managed to provide an optimum environment for wintering waterfowl. The water impoundments (pools) on the East Dike route are kept clear of overgrowth. In contrast, the Barbour Hill area is the only area within False Cape State Park kept clear of overgrowth for waterfowl. The Barbour Hill area is managed cooperatively by Back Bay National Wildlife Refuge and False Cape State Park. The remainder of False Cape State Park is a dense, undeveloped habitat filled with loblolly pine, gum, maple and oak trees.

Hunt clubs originally occupied both areas. Due to the abundance of waterfowl, hunters from within and outside the state gravitated to this area beginning in the late 1800's. In 1938, hunting was curtailed with the establishment of the Back Bay National Wildlife Refuge. At that time, the acreage of the refuge consisted of 4,589 acres within the refuge. By the Presidential Proclamation of 1939, a total of 4,600 acres were set aside as a protected area for migratory birds.

From the beginning, those managing the refuge have worked to provide an advantageous environment for the many birds that make this area their winter home. From November 1 until April 1, the water impoundment areas of the refuge are closed to visitors to ensure that the wintering waterfowl are not disturbed. Studies have shown that in order for the birds to return to the north and to reproduce, they must have an environment conducive to resting and feeding. When humans, on foot or in vehicles, pass a water impoundment, the flock of birds resting there is apt to fly into the air, circle then come to rest again. This action wastes precious energy, negating their feeding efforts. Therefore, the refuge limits the proximity of visitors during the wintering time.

It was recognized early on that urban development was quickly consuming available wetlands important to the preservation of many species of birds and wildlife. Therefore, the national refuge efforts to preserve this land are important. To this end, continual maintenance of the various environments of the refuge is necessary. A major rehabilitation program was started in the late 1980's and finished in 1994. For this program, a sum of $750,000 was committed to elevate the dikes in order to increase the depth of the water impoundments and to add water control structures. In 1986, the United States and Canada signed the North American Waterfowl Management Plan to increase the dwindling numbers of waterfowl and other wildlife dependent on the wetlands. Other maintenance techniques include burning off shrubs that infringe on the marshes, discing (which is a technique that stimulates plant growth in the ponds by stirring up pond bottoms), and deliberately disturbing select areas to prevent growth of woody plants. They also drastically lower the water levels periodically to replenish the plant life in the water impoundments, so there will be plenty of food for the birds. All of these techniques are designed to support the waterfowl that winter here.

Today, the refuge is home to thousands of migrating geese, ducks, and swans as well as many other species of birds and wildlife. In late fall, the welcome sound of honking geese or quacking ducks, fills the air as birds arrive in their winter home in large flocks. Birders from everywhere frequent the refuge for a glimpse of the many birds that winter here. But, don't forget about the other wildlife of the area. Reptiles and amphibians as well as river otters, white-tailed deer, raccoons, gray fox, muskrats, rabbits, and mink call the refuge home. It is not unusual to see feral pigs scurrying through the marsh with piglets close behind. Also, endangered species, such as loggerhead turtles, piping plovers, peregrine falcons, and bald eagles are protected by the refuge.

When the refuge is fully open in spring, summer and early fall, you can walk the 4.25 mile East Dike route to False Cape State Park. When the refuge is closed, you can only reach the False Cape State Park by boat or by walking approximately 4 miles down the beach. At times, ground transportation is offered to False Cape from the Visitor Contact Station at Back Bay. Be sure to call ahead to check on this.

A visit to the undeveloped setting of False Cape State Park makes you appreciate how difficult the primitive life of those who lived in Wash Woods in the late 1800s must have been. False Cape derived it's name from appearing similar to Cape Henry from the sea. Fooled by the appearance of the False Cape shoreline, sailors would steer their ships as if to enter the Chesapeake Bay. By the time they realized that they were 20 miles too far south, it was too late. As a consequence, many of them ran aground in this area of the coast.

Wash Woods, a community of approximately 300 at its peak, grew up within the area known as False Cape State Park because two life-saving stations, False Cape Life-Saving Station in Virginia and Wash Woods Station across the border in North Carolina, were located on this section of the coast to save lives during the many shipwrecks. One shipwreck resulted in the building of the Wash Woods Methodist Church. The church is said to have been built from the cypress that was the cargo of the schooner, James S. Woods, that went aground on the coast in 1889. The Wash Woods community was so primitive, it could not entice a minister to take up residence there for Wash Woods Methodist Church. Instead, ministers for the church came in on horseback or by boat from Princess Anne County.

The inhabitants of Wash Woods survived by hunting, fishing and some farming, but their life was difficult. During storms, for example, with the barrier spit only 2 miles from bay to ocean at the widest, the Wash Woods area was covered with water and sand. When hunting dwindled, many left the area. The state began purchasing the land in the 1960's and established it as False Cape State Park. It opened in 1980.

Since there is no drinkable water and there are only primitive campsites and pit toilets within the park, you need to plan ahead for a walk in False Cape State Park. It is well worth the effort, however, because the area is undeveloped, and you'll see some breathtaking sites that you won't see anywhere else.

Both areas present many educational programs. Moonlight canoe trips, snake lectures, loggerhead sea turtle programs, and bird watching expeditions are just a few of the offerings throughout the year..

Walks
This is the perfect spot to design your own walk. Check the map and choose the environments you want to visit and the distance you wish to walk.

Back Bay National Wildlife Refuge Walks

1. *Bay Trail (.4 miles one way):* The Bay Trail starts behind the Back Bay Visitor Contact Station. It takes you through the marsh habitat to a spectacular view of Sand Bay.

2. *Seaside Trail (.25 miles one way):* This boardwalk starts beside the Back Bay Visitor Contact Station. It takes you over the dunes to the beach.

3. *Dune Trail (.5 miles one way):* This elevated boardwalk starts to the left a short way down the East Dike gravel road. It is an elevated boardwalk over marsh and dunes to the beach. You can combine the Seaside Trail and the Dune Trail by taking one out to the beach and the other back.

4. *East Dike (4.25 miles one way):* This gravel road starts beside the Back Bay Visitor Contact Station and winds past the dike system and water impoundments to False Cape State Park. Be

sure to watch your mileage and turn around and return to the parking area when you have gone the distance you desire. On it you'll pass the water impoundments where waterfowl winter. As you walk closer to False Cape State Park, notice the nesting boxes for wood ducks. This species almost disappeared, but humans compensated by building nesting boxes that have a guard partway up the base to prevent predators from reaching the nests.

False Cape State Park Walks

The directions for False Cape State Park walks assume that you are walking the main hiking/biking trail from north to south.

1. **Barbour Hill Interpretive Trail (2.4 miles one way):** There are 24 learning stations that correspond to information in a booklet on this square loop. It starts at the border of Back Bay and False Cape. There is an overlook on the trail that is a perfect spot to photograph waterfowl or for a panoramic view of the area.

2. **Barbour Hill Beach Trail (.7 miles one way):** This trail intersects the main hiking/biking trail. Turn left onto the trail. It will take you to the unspoiled beach.

3. **South Inlet Trail (.4 miles one way):** The South Inlet Trail walk also intersects the main hiking/biking trail. Turn right onto the trail. It will take you to the Back Bay side of False Cape. This is also a good spot for photography. Volunteers built the overlook for this trail

4. **False Cape Landing Trail (.6 miles one way):** The False Cape Landing Trail leads in both directions from the main hiking/biking trail. To the right, it leads to the False Cape Landing area of Back Bay, and to the left, it takes you to the beach.

5. **Wash Woods Beach Trail (.8 miles one way):** This trail also cuts across False Cape from the bay to the ocean.

6. **Wash Woods Interpretive Trail (.7 miles one way):** The Wash Woods Interpretive Trail leads from the area of the Wash Woods

Environmental Education Center to the beach. This trail also interprets the environment.

7. *Cemetery Trail (.5 miles one way):* The Cemetery Trail intersects the Wash Woods Interpretive Trail about mid-point and leads to the Wash Woods Cemetery and Church sites.

8. *Dudley Island Trail (3 miles one way):* Dudley Island Trail leads from the end of the main hiking/biking trail to the beach at the south end of False Cape State Park.

9. *Main Hiking/Biking Trail (4.3 miles one way):* The main hiking/biking trail cuts a path through False Cape State Park from north to south to the Dudley Island Trail.

Point of Interest

Wash Woods Methodist Church: Remnants of the Wash Woods Methodist Church and a portion of its steeple can be seen on the church site in the Wash Woods area of False Cape State Park.

First Landing/Seashore State Park

Key

●	Contact Station
P	Parking
?	Visitor Center
🚻	Restrooms
▬	Park Road
- - -	Trail
✕	Picnic Area

Walks

Trail	Miles	Trail Markers
Cape Henry	6.0	Dark Green
Long Creek	5.0	Orange
Osprey	1.2	Green
Bald Cypress	1.5	Red
Osmanthus	2.4	Blue
Kingfisher	0.6	White
Fox Run	0.3	Yellow
White Hill Lake	1.4	Gold

First Landing/Seashore State Park

Description

First Landing/Seashore State Park is the perfect setting to devise your own walk in a truly remarkable setting. The park consists of 19 miles of well-maintained and well-marked trails that allow visitors the opportunity to experience a variety of environments, including beach, dune, marsh, and woods. An abundance of rich foliage and variety of wildlife make this site one nature lovers won't want to miss. Sub-tropical bald cypress trees with Spanish moss hanging from their branches mix with the more temperate American olive and water oak on many of the trails. Trails carve a path through low lands, a boardwalk meanders deep inside cypress ponds, and dense woods shade the trails. The opportunities to observe egrets, heron, osprey, and numerous other species of birds are endless. Allow time to sit and listen to the sounds of nature on one of the many benches in the park.

Location

First Landing/Seashore State Park is located in Virginia Beach. The main entrance to it is on Shore Drive with an alternate entrance off Atlantic Ave. at 64th Street.

Main Entrance (Shore Drive): From I-64, take Northampton Blvd. (Rt. 13) toward the Chesapeake Bay Bridge Tunnel. Follow Northampton Blvd. to the last exit before the Chesapeake Bay Bridge Tunnel, which is the Shore Drive - Rt. 60 exit. Bear to the right off the exit onto Shore Drive - Rt. 60 East. Follow Shore Drive over the Lynnhaven Inlet bridge. The entrance to First Landing/Seashore State Park is approximately 4.5 miles from the Shore Drive turn off. Turn right into the entrance to the park.

Main Entrance (Shore Drive): From the Virginia Beach ocean front, follow Atlantic Avenue north to where it joins with Shore Drive (just after 82nd Street). Bear left onto Shore Drive. Watch for the entrance to the park on your left approximately 4 miles down the road.

Alternate Entrance (64th Street): There is also an entrance at the south end of the park at the Contact Station at 64th street. From I-64, follow the above directions and go past the main entrance to the park on Shore Drive. Follow Shore Drive and bear right onto Atlantic Avenue. Follow Atlantic Avenue south and turn right onto 64th Street (the 64th Street entrance is approximately 5.5 miles from the Shore Drive entrance to the park).

Alternate Entrance (64th Street): From the Virginia Beach oceanfront, follow Atlantic Avenue north and turn left onto 64th Street.

Parking and Facilities
There is parking at the Contact Station off Shore Drive, at the Visitor Center, at the south end of the park at the Contact Station at 64th Street, and at the Narrows Boat Ramp at the end of 64th Street. Restrooms are located at the Visitor Center, the picnic area, and the parking lot at the Narrows. Camping is also available at First Landing/Seashore State Park. The park is open from dawn to dusk daily. There is a parking fee.

Safety Tip
Changes to the park trails are possible due to weather conditions; therefore, it is a good idea to check at the Visitor Center regarding the current condition of the trails.

Background
Today, the total acreage for First Landing/Seashore State Park is 2,770. It began with a gift of 1,064 acres in 1933, two years after that the Virginia Seashore State Park Association was formed. Shortly thereafter, another 2,373 acres were added from Cape Henry, but in World War II the area that is now Fort Story was reclaimed by the government to protect the coast.

In 1933, the Civilian Conservation Corps began building trails, camping and cabin areas, and administrative sites. The current Visitor Center was built in 1981. The park hosts approximately one million guests each year.

First Landing/Seashore State Park is unique because it is the northern-most location on the east coast where sub-tropical and temperate plants mingle in the same location. The beauty of the Spanish moss is an example of plant life that reaches its northern-most point here. There is not only a variety of plants to see in this natural setting, but there is also a variety of environments, including beach, woods, marsh, and dune areas.

Walks

First Landing/Seashore State Park contains 19 miles of trails. This is the perfect location to design your own walking route depending on the length you want to walk and the environments you want to explore.

1. *Cape Henry Trail (6.0 miles - dark green markers):* There are three parts to Cape Henry Trail. It is a wide trail and doubles as a bike path, so stay to the side and watch for bikes coming up behind you. Because Cape Henry Trail extends the length of the park, it offers a variety of walking environments. You'll walk through dune areas and bald cypress swamps. After you cross 64th Street and continue toward the Narrows, you'll use a wooden bridge to cross a salt marsh. Osprey nests can be viewed in this area.

    a) The first part of Cape Henry Trail (1.0 mile) extends from the Shore Drive Contact Station area to the Visitor Center. There is a picnic area about a quarter of a mile along the trail.

    b) The second part of Cape Henry Trail (3.4 miles) extends from the Visitor Center to 64th Street. There are benches located at .75 miles, at approximately 2 miles, and at 2.3 miles from the Visitor Center for rest periods and to enjoy the scenery.

    c) The third part of Cape Henry Trail (1.5) begins at the 64th Street Contact Station to the Narrows Boat Ramp. On this portion of the trail, you will walk along a manmade lake. There are benches along the way where you can enjoy wonderful views of the lake, the marsh, or Broad Bay.

2. *Long Creek Trail (5.0 miles - orange markers):*
    *   If you park in the parking lot at the Shore Drive Contact Station, walk on the road (toward the Visitor Center) .3 miles and turn right onto Long Creek Trail.

    *   If you park at the Visitor Center, walk back toward the picnic area and cut across Fox Run Trail (.6 miles) and turn left onto Long Creek Trail.

Long Creek Trail starts at the road between the picnic area and the Visitor Center and continues to 64th Street. Due to several dunes, Long Creek Trail is the most hilly of the trails. White Hill Lake is visible from the trail. This is a good place to observe osprey because they nest around the lake. The variety of environments (forest, beach, dunes, marshes) makes it a varied walk. When crossing the marshes, watch for egrets and great blue herons. Because this is a long walk if you must return to the picnic parking area or the Visitor Center parking area, you may want to go only part way on this trail then double back. At 1.7 miles into the walk, you'll come to the junction of White Hill Lake Trail. Bear to the right to stay on Long Creek Trail. If you choose to take White Hill Lake Trail, it will take you (1.4 miles) to Cape Henry Trail. At 2.1 miles on Long Creek Trail is the juncture with Osprey Trail. To the left is Long Creek Trail, and Osprey Trail continues to the right. Osprey Trail meets Long Creek Trail again at 3.4 miles. When you reach 64th Street, it is .6 miles to the Contact Station on 64th Street. When planning this walk with a friend, one idea is to park a car at each end of it so you can walk the entire trail without having to double back.

3. *Osprey Trail (1.2 miles - green markers):* Osprey Trail begins and ends on Long Creek Trail. Osprey Trail is subject to flooding at high tide. This trail provides a beautiful view of Broad Bay as well as the tranquility of cypress swamps.

4. *Bald Cypress Trail (1.5 miles - red markers):* This trail is a popular one due to its proximity to the Visitor Center and the scenery. It begins near the Visitor Center. The trail proceeds immediately into an area rich with Spanish moss and bald cypress trees. At .3 miles, the Osmanthus Trail comes in from the left. Bear to the right to stay on Bald Cypress Trail and continue to walk the back half of Bald Cypress Trail. The Visitor Center has written materials (for a small fee) about this trail that give details about plant life, trees, and points of interest marked on the trail by red numbers. There are a couple of inclines on the trail, but it is mostly level. Numerous boardwalks and benches provide places to stop and enjoy the view of the cypress swamp or to watch for wildlife.

5. *Osmanthus Trail (2.4 miles - blue markers):* There is no way to reach this trial except to follow the Bald Cypress Trail. Osmanthus Trail starts at the .7 mile point on the Bald Cypress Trail. The trail is named for the Osmanthus americanus, which is Latin for American olive tree. An example of this tree can be seen at the juncture of the Bald Cypress Trial and the Osmanthus Trail and along the trail. In addition, there are many other varieties of trees in the forest, including red maple, beech, water oak, black oak, sassafras, and holly. The environment of this trail is wet as it is carved through lowlands. At the halfway point in the trail, you will cross a footbridge. At times, there is a stream under this bridge. Shortly into the second half of the trail, you will walk over a 200 foot boardwalk over the lagoon. Another boardwalk at 1.8 miles spans a larger lagoon. Once you complete the circle, either turn right or left on Bald Cypress Trail and return to the Visitor Center.

6. *Kingfisher Trail (.6 miles - white markers):* Kingfisher Trail is a .6 mile trail that connects the Cape Henry Trail and Long Creek Trail. It meets Cape Henry Trail at 1.25 miles from the Visitor Center. It is a high, dry trail with shade provided by American beech trees.

7. *Fox Run Trail (.3 miles - yellow markers):* Fox Run Trail is to your right from the Visitor Center. It is a short walk and connects the Visitor Center road and the Long Creek Trail. This

trail, although short, is a good one for bird watchers. The trail was named for the gray fox. Foxes are seldom sited on or near the trail, but they do live in this area of the park.

8. *White Hill Lake Trail (1.4 miles - gold markers):* White Hill Lake Trail begins 1.7 miles along the Long Creek Trail from the Visitor Center and ends at the Cape Henry Trail. On Cape Henry Trail, it is 1.1 miles to the right to reach the Contact Station at 64th Street and 2.4 miles to the left to reach the Visitor Center. This wide trail winds past several cypress ponds and you can see American beeches and sweet gum trees from the trail.

Points of Interest

1. *Visitor Center:* The Visitor Center is a good starting point for any outing. It contains a nature display. This is one of four starting points for a self-designed hike. The park staff often conduct walks to educate park goers about the wildlife and plant life that can be seen in the park. Check at the Visitor Center for topics and times.

2. *Camping:* Beach campsites and cabins are available on the one mile beach on the Chesapeake Bay. The main park has camping and cabins in wooded areas. Reservations are required for both sites. During tourist season (Memorial Day through Labor Day), the beach is only open to registered guests.

3. *Picnic Area:* A picnic area is located between the Contact Station off Shore Drive and the Visitor Center. There are grills available at the picnic area.

Fort Story

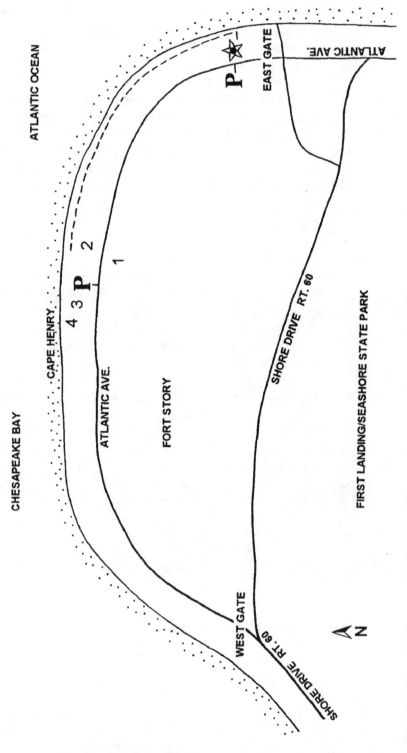

Key

P Parking

✦ Start Here

- - - - Walk

1) Old Cape Henry Lighthouse
2) Cape Henry Lighthouse
3) Battle of the Capes Monument/Overlook
4) First Landing

Description

This is one of the most historically significant sites in American history. Fort Story is a perfect location for a memorable beach walk. This vast undeveloped beach front, which stretches along the Atlantic coast at the north end of Virginia Beach, is where those under the command of Captain Christopher Newport first landed on April 26, 1607. A small memorial park and overlook here are dedicated to those who made the arduous journey so long ago. The towering lighthouses remind us of how dangerous this coastline was for ships. Today, Fort Story is a 1,451 acre military base at the point where the Atlantic Ocean meets the Chesapeake Bay. On the beach, you'll see sandpipers scurrying after waves, and if you look closely, you'll catch sight of a sandcrab tentatively venturing out of his sand tunnel. Be sure to watch the horizon for ships and pleasure boats rounding the cape into the Chesapeake Bay. Dolphin are frequently spotted feeding on schools of small fish in the summer months, and whales, too, can be seen from the shore feeding in the winter. This is a beach walk unlike any other. As you stroll along the pristine beach, you will see the lighthouses jutting from behind the dunes.

Location

From I-64, take the Rt. 44 East exit and follow Rt. 44 to Atlantic Avenue at the oceanfront. Turn left onto Atlantic Avenue and follow it to Fort Story. At the light where Shore Drive veers off to the left, bear to the right to the gate at Fort Story. After going through the base gate, turn left into the parking area. A walkway to the beach is directly across Atlantic Avenue from the parking lot.

Parking and Facilities

Parking is available just inside the Fort Story gate on Atlantic Avenue and also at the Old Cape Henry Lighthouse.

Background

The history of Cape Henry began years before the Fort Story military base was established. On April 26, 1607, Christopher Newport sent 24 men ashore here. He had sailed three ships (the Godspeed, the Susan Constant, and the Discovery) from England to establish the first English settlement in the new world. This historic event was the first landing of English settlers on American soil. Soon after landing, Captain Newport sent the exploration party ashore to locate a site for the settlement. The party was attacked by the Chesapeake Indians, causing Newport to decide the area would be too difficult to defend against attack to be a good location for a settlement.

On April 29th, the ships sailed into what is now the Chesapeake Bay then up the James River and established the first English colony at Jamestown Island. Before leaving to search for a more suitable location for the settlement, they placed a cross at the spot, which they named Cape Henry after the Prince of Wales. With the placement of the cross, they laid claim to the land for England and held the first religious service of the Church of England in America.

During the Revolutionary War, the Battle of the Capes occurred at this site in 1781. The French were victorious over the British. This battle paved the way for the later battle at Yorktown which was the definitive battle of the war.

For years, a lighthouse was proposed for Cape Henry to decrease the number of shipwrecks off the coast. One of the first acts of the first congress after the Revolutionary War was to create a lighthouse service. Construction of the Cape Henry Lighthouse began in 1791. In 1872, cracks were found in the lighthouse, and in 1881, the new lighthouse was built 350 feet southeast of the old one. Both still stand today.

The area became a military base in 1914 when the General Assembly offered the land to the federal government. It was named Fort Story after General John Patton Story who was an artilleryman.

During World War I, Fort Story became part of the coast defenses of the Chesapeake Bay. In 1925, it became the Harbor Defense

Footsteps:

Command, and in 1941 it became the Headquarters of the Harbor Defense Command.

During World War II, Fort Story became home to a hospital for those returning from the war. The hospital closed two years later after serving 13,472 patients.

After the war, Fort Story became an amphibious training center, and it was transferred to the Transportation Training Command of Fort Eustis in Newport News. Today, it continues to serve as an installation of Fort Eustis.

Walk

The beach walk at Fort Story is as long or as short as you want to make it. From the parking area, cross Atlantic Avenue and take the path to the beach. Turn left onto the beach and walk as far as you desire. Do not try to reach the Points of Interest from the beach.

Points of Interest

There is no beach access to the Points of Interest. You must use the parking lot near the sites on Atlantic Avenue.

1. *Old Cape Henry Lighthouse:* In 1627, the General Assembly recommended that a lighthouse be built at Cape Henry, but colonists were too busy with their own survival to build a structure. A lighthouse was recommended again in 1727 by the House of Burgesses, but again it was not built. When the first congress met after the Revolutionary War, an act was passed to create a lighthouse service in an attempt to decrease the number of shipwrecks along the Atlantic coast. Construction of the lighthouse finally began in 1791. In addition to the lighthouse, a frame house was built for the keeper of the light and a vault was constructed to store the oil for the light. The first keeper of the light was Laban Goffigan. The light was lit for the first time in October of 1792. When the new lighthouse was completed in 1881, Old Cape Henry Lighthouse was not torn down as it provided a landmark during daylight. On April 29, 1896, the Association for the Preservation of Virginia Antiquities placed a marker commemorating the first landing of the English at this site. The lighthouse is the oldest lighthouse

built by the government and is visited by at least 30,000 yearly. There is a fee to tour the Old Cape Henry Lighthouse.

2. *Cape Henry Lighthouse:* During an inspection of the old lighthouse in 1872, cracks were found. It took repeated requests for replacement of the lighthouse before money was appropriated in 1878. The new lighthouse was completed in 1881. It is located 350 feet southeast of the old one.

3. *Battle of the Capes Monument:* This site consists of the monument, an overlook, and plaques to commemorate the battle of 1781 that took place here. The French were victorious over the British in that battle.

4. *First Landing:* A cross was placed by Christopher Newport and his men to mark the spot where the first English settlers first landed after their long voyage to America. After exploring the area for a couple of days in April of 1607, they moved onto Jamestown Island where they established the first English settlement.

Virginia Beach Boardwalk

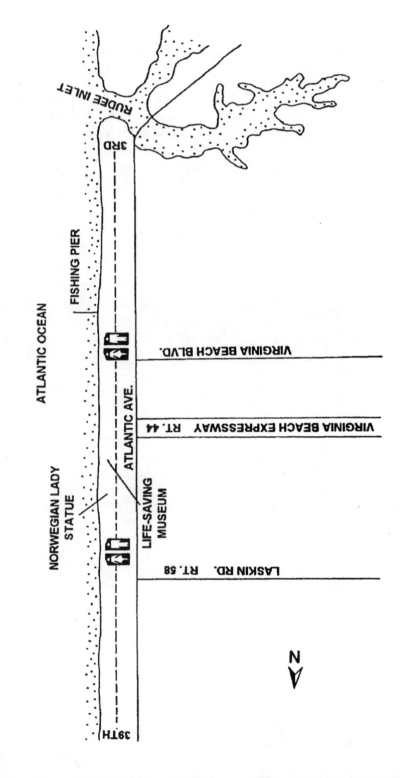

Key

 Restrooms

- - - Walk

Description

Ocean waves breaking on shore, swimmers wading or body surfing, dolphin performing off shore as they swim in schools, fishermen dropping a line from the 15th Street pier, surfers trying to catch that perfect wave, cyclists and in-line skaters whizzing by on the bike path, tourists sipping a cool drink on the balcony of a high rise hotel, waitresses serving coffee at outdoor cafes, historic buildings mixed in with the modern hotels, and lifeguards keeping watch from their chairs mounted on high platforms.... These are the sights and sounds of the Virginia Beach Boardwalk.

If you're looking for a walk by the ocean with a definite tourist slant, the Virginia Beach Boardwalk is the spot for you. The boardwalk is 2.4 miles long and you can start your walk anywhere from 3rd Street to 39th Street. There are stairs spaced at regular intervals along the way to offer you the choice to walk on the beach at any point.

Walking along the boardwalk blends the old and the new. In one block, you might pass a new high-rise hotel and in the next an original beach house. The boardwalk is carefully landscaped and benches offer a chance to sit and watch the ocean and all the activity along the boardwalk.

Location

To reach the boardwalk, take I-64 to Rt. 44 East. Follow Rt. 44 to the oceanfront.

Parking and Facilities

Public parking is available in the vicinity of 3rd Street and Atlantic, on 19th Street between Arctic Avenue and Pacific Avenue, and on 18th Street between Arctic Avenue and Pacific Avenue. There are also many other parking lots available. Fees for parking vary. Public restrooms are available near the boardwalk at 17th St. and at 30th St. Parallel to the boardwalk is a bike path for cyclists and in-line skaters. Both bikes and skates are available on the boardwalk for rental.

Background

The vast area of Virginia Beach we know today wasn't created as such until 1963. Before that, it was known as Princess Anne County. The section known as Virginia Beach in the early days consisted only of a quiet village at the coast.

Powhatan was the chief of the Powhatan Confederacy, a group of at least 30 tribes of Indians who inhabited eastern Virginia. The Chesapeake Indians were part of the Powhatan Confederacy and were the first known to live in the area now called Virginia Beach. In the 1500's, Powhatan's priests told him that a nation would rise from the east. Unfortunately, he interpreted this to mean that the Chesapeake Indians were going to rise against him. So, Powhatan attacked the Chesapeake Indians and very few were left when the killing was over.

In 1586, Sir Walter Raleigh (for whom the Raleigh Tavern in Williamsburg is named) set out to relocate the Roanoke Island settlement. He sent Sir Ralph Lane and a company of men on an exploration in search of a suitable piece of land. When they landed on the Atlantic Coast, they met no resistance in going ashore in the vicinity of Virginia Beach because the Chesapeake Indians had not regained their numbers.

On April 26, 1607, Christopher Newport sailed the Godspeed, the Susan Constant, and the Discovery from England to establish the first English settlement. They first landed at Cape Henry in Virginia Beach. Newport sent 24 men ashore to explore the area but determined that it was too vulnerable to attacks by the Spanish or Indians, especially after the Chesapeake Indians attacked his men.

Newport sailed the three ships up the James River and chose the site at the island of Jamestown for the settlement. Fourteen years later, some of the colonists returned to Virginia Beach to settle.

The area of Virginia Beach/Princess Anne County grew slowly. Adam Thoroughgood, a tobacco farmer, was one of the first settlers of the area where Lynnhaven is now. In 1635, he gained ownership of 5,350 acres. The next year, he built his home on the Lynnhaven River. The Lynnhaven House remains today and is one of the oldest houses in the country.

In August of 1637, another group of settlers, this time 500 in all, sailed for the colonies. The trip was a perilous one. The captain, a crew member, and 60 passengers perished during the Atlantic crossing. In January of 1638, the ship anchored off Lynnhaven. Some of the crew ventured ashore in search of provisions. During the night, the weather turned bad and high seas pushed the ship onto the shore. Many passengers lost their lives. Those who struggled to shore could not find adequate shelter and many more perished. In all, only approximately one third of the original 500 survived. This story made others more cautious in making a decision to sail for the colonies.

Throughout the years, the areas of Virginia Beach and Princess Anne County became known for several historical facts. For instance, the famous pirate, Blackbeard, who plundered many ships during the early 1700's had his headquarters in Virginia Beach. Another bit of history is that Witchduck Road was named because Grace Sherwood, who was thought to be a witch, was marched down the road to the Lynnhaven River in July of 1706 for a public dunking. She failed the dunking test because she did not sink. Therefore she was jailed for being a witch. Witchduck Point is the name of the site of her dunking.

Princess Anne County saw little fighting during the Revolutionary War; however, one of the first skirmishes of the war was said to have taken place on November 16, 1775 in the Kempsville area. In 1781, the French engaged the British in the Battle of the Capes at Cape Henry where Fort Story is today. The French were victorious.

After the Civil War, the area began reconstruction projects. To attract people to the beach, Virginia Beach constructed a clubhouse at 17th and Oceanfront in 1880. Around the same time, the Virginia Beach Hotel was built to accommodate 75 guests. It was lavishly decorated and enlarged in 1887 to accommodate 400 visitors. It was also renamed as the Princess Anne Hotel. Many famous people stayed at this luxury hotel, including President Harrison and President Cleveland. Alexander Graham Bell also stayed here. In 1907, the hotel burned but was rebuilt in 1922.

Virginia Beach saw growth and action during World War I and World War II. Fort Story was established in 1914 and was heavily fortified to protect the vital Chesapeake Bay and the surrounding land. During World War I three more military bases were added to the Virginia Beach and Princess Anne County area. In 1945, Little Creek Amphibious base was the result of the consolidation of four smaller bases. Today, a drive down Shore Drive reveals an impressive array of ships.

During World War II, German U-boats patrolled off the coast of Virginia Beach and are responsible for sinking allied ships. Due to this threat, trade slowed but shipments of war supplies grew.

Major growth occurred post-war. When the resort at Virginia Beach annexed Princess Anne County in 1963, the population was 125,000. In 1970, the population was 172,106 and by 1990 grew to 393,069. The resort industry is still very important to the area and is the reason that Virginia Beach takes such care in preserving the beaches and the boardwalk.

Walk
The boardwalk is 2.4 miles in length. You can start anywhere along the way and stop when you want. In addition, if you want a longer walk, you can venture onto the beach and walk for miles.

Points of Interest
1. *Rudee Inlet:* Charter boats originate in this area. Near the beginning of the boardwalk at Rudee Inlet, the marinas offer many fishing excursions or tours to see the sights from offshore. The whale and dolphin watching expeditions that leave from the inlet are very popular.

2. *15th Street Fishing Pier:* The pier is open 24 hours a day. There is a small fee if you want to visit or fish from the pier. If you're

interested in fishing, you can rent a rod and purchase bait at the pier.

3. *Life-Saving Museum of Virginia (24th Street and Atlantic Avenue):* This structure is a Virginia Historic Museum on the National Register of Historic Places. It houses a gift shop and museum. It was built in 1903 and depicts the valiant efforts of life-saving patrols to rescue victims of the many shipwrecks that occurred off the coast. A guided tour shows the development of life-saving equipment and methods over the years. In addition, the museum contains a display that chronicles the history of the involvement of Virginia Beach in WWI and WWII.

4. *Norwegian Lady Statue (25th Street and Oceanfront):* This bronze statue was a gift from the people of Moss, Norway in memory of those who lost their lives in the shipwreck in 1891 of the Norwegian ship, The Dictator. The statue is also dedicated to the life-saving crew who managed, against the odds, to save 10 sailors.

Points of Interest in the Vicinity

1. *Atlantic Wildfowl Heritage Center (113 Atlantic Avenue):* This gallery opened in 1995. It is managed by the Back Bay Wildfowl Guild and displays 5 galleries of artwork and decoys, both old and new.

2. *Babes and Bears Toy Museum (209 29th Street between Atlantic and Pacific avenues):* This museum displays 3,000 dolls and 1,500 stuffed bears in scenes or in groups with like creatures. It started as a family collection that grew too large, so the owner decided to share the collection with the public.

3. *Virginia Marine Science Museum (717 General Booth Boulevard):* This unique museum displays all facets of marine life that live in and around the waters of Virginia. A 50,000 gallon aquarium is always a big attraction. There is a boardwalk through a salt marsh that connects the buildings of the museum. It's truly a thorough exhibit of marine life and well worth a visit. There is an entrance fee.

The sign reads:

WASHINGTON DITCH

SURVEYED BY GEORGE WASHINGTON IN 1763. A CART ROAD WAS BUILT FIRST ALONG THIS 4½ MILE DITCH AND THE CANAL DUG ALONGSIDE BY SLAVE LABOR FOR TRANSPORTATION. GRESHAM NIMMO, UNDER THE PERSONAL DIRECTION OF GEORGE WASHINGTON, DID THE SURVEYING AND KEPT THE NOTES.

Great Dismal Swamp

Chippokes Plantation State Park

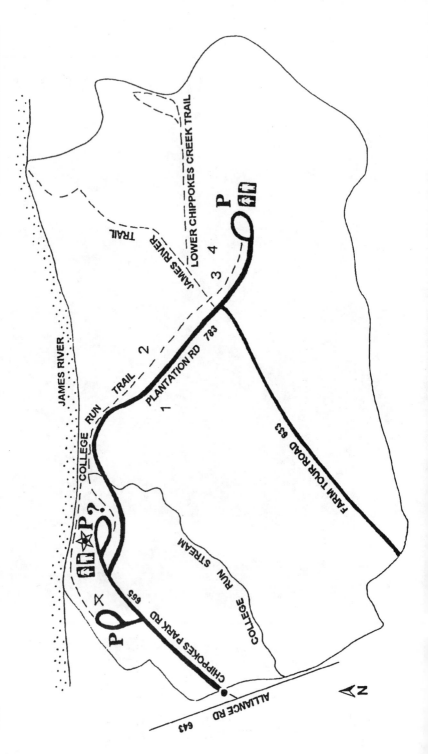

Key

- • Contact Station
- ? Visitor Center
- P Parking
- 🚻 Restrooms
- ✦ Start Here
- --·-- Trail
- ✕ Picnic Area
- ▬ Park Road

Walks

		Trail	Miles
1)	Farm & Forestry Museum & Sawmill Exhibit		
2)	River House	Lower Chippokes Creek	1.0
3)	Mansion	James River	0.9
4)	Paradise Gardens	College Run	1.3

Footsteps: ————————————————————————

Chippokes Plantation State Park

Description

Chippokes Plantation State Park sits quietly on the banks of the James River near Surry. The south bank of the James River borders one side of Chippokes Plantation for two miles. The eastern border of the plantation is the Lower Chippokes Creek, and to the west, it is bordered by the College Run Stream. The park offers three trails through the plantation, ranging from .9 miles to 1.3 miles in length. You can choose the College Run Trail and walk the route that farmers took in colonial days to roll barrels of tobacco and grain to the shoreline where the goods were floated to English merchant ships. If you prefer a walk with the opportunity to enjoy wildlife, you can follow the path (James River Trail) from the mansion through the open fields of the farm, then enter a wooded area opening onto the tidal marshes along the James River. Or, you can choose to walk the Lower Chippokes Creek Trail, where you can watch for barn swallows, bobwhites, quail, deer, opossum and racoons as you leave the farm road and walk to a loop overlooking the tidal marshes at Lower Chippokes Creek. These diverse routes offer walkers an opportunity to tour the plantation, learning its history and developing an appreciation of the complexity and diversity of its operation in the process. Chippokes is the oldest continuously working farm in North America, and its meticulous presentation makes this site a unique walking experience.

Location

Chippokes Plantation State Park is located near Surry, Virginia. Follow Rt. 10 north to Rt. 634 (Alliance Rd.). Turn right onto Rt. 634 then left into the park. There is a fee at the Contact Station.

Parking and Facilities

Parking, information, and restroom facilities are available at the Visitor Center. Additional parking and restrooms are available near the Farm and Forestry Museum and Sawmill Exhibit on College Run Trail and behind the mansion near the start of the James River Trail and the Lower Chippokes Creek Trail. The park is closed a couple of times per year for deer hunting; therefore, it's good to call ahead.

Background

The history of Chippokes Plantation dates back to 1612, although it wasn't until 1616 that it was formally recognized as a plantation. It is the oldest continuously working farm in North America. Captain William Powell, who served in the first House of Burgesses, was the first owner of 800 acres of the 1600 acre plantation. He named the plantation after Choupocke, an Indian chief who was friendly to the Jamestown settlers. (The name of the plantation has been spelled several different ways over the years, but "Chippokes" is the current spelling.)

When Captain Powell was massacred by Indians in 1622, his son, George Powell, inherited the land. When George Powell died in 1643, ownership of the land reverted to the Crown. The Crown granted the land plus the additional 800 acres to Governor Sir William Berkeley. When he died, his wife inherited the land. Her third husband was Phillip Ludwell, and Chippokes plantation stayed in the Ludwell family for 5 generations until 1837.

In 1838, Albert Carroll Jones purchased the plantation. For several years, he lived in the farm house on College Run, but in 1854, he built the mansion and the adjacent buildings. For the next few decades, Chippokes Plantation stayed in the Jones family. In 1918, it was sold to Mr. and Mrs. Victor Stewart at a public auction. The size of Chippokes at that time was 1403 acres. After Mr. Stewart died, Mrs. Stewart gave the plantation to the Commonwealth of Virginia in 1967 to preserve it as a learning center for the history of agriculture in Virginia.

Walks

1. *College Run Trail (1.3 miles one way):* Beginning at the Visitor Center, College Run Trail leads along the James River past the River House and the Farm and Forestry Museum and Sawmill

Exhibit to the mansion. It is designed for walkers and bikers and is a paved flat surface.

2. *James River Trail (.9 miles one way):* The James River Trail begins at the mansion. Take the road in front of the mansion and follow it through the farmland and a wooded area to the shore of the James River. Walkers can go the entire length of the trail and down a steep hill to the James River. Bikers also use part of this trail.

3. *Lower Chippokes Creek Trail (1 mile one way):* The Lower Chippokes Creek Trail begins at the side of the mansion. It follows a farm road then enters a woodland path to a loop overlooking a tidal marsh.

Points of Interest

1. *Farm and Forestry Museum and Sawmill Exhibit:* The exhibit tells the story of early farm life from building the farm to harvesting crops. Also, there are exhibits and artifacts of professions that served to support the operation of the farm, such as blacksmith, wheelwright and cobbler tools. The display shows the improvements made in the implements used by these craftsmen over the years.

2. *River House:* The 19th century frame house probably served as a secondary dwelling while the Ludwells owned the plantation. Near it are several farm buildings essential to the operation of the plantation.

3 *Mansion:* The mansion stands in prominent view from the James River and the white front served as a guide to vessels in the river by day and by night. At night, lanterns were lit on the lawn to illuminate it. The cupola on top provides a clear view of the plantation and the boat landing. Separate buildings to the side and back of the mansion housed the kitchen, a gardener's cottage, and a carriage house. The mansion is an example of middle class living of the day.

4. *Paradise Gardens:* Mrs. Victor Stewart built the gardens behind the mansion. She designed them to bloom year round by gathering plants from around the world. The plants are labeled and color-coded for easy identification according to the season they bloom.

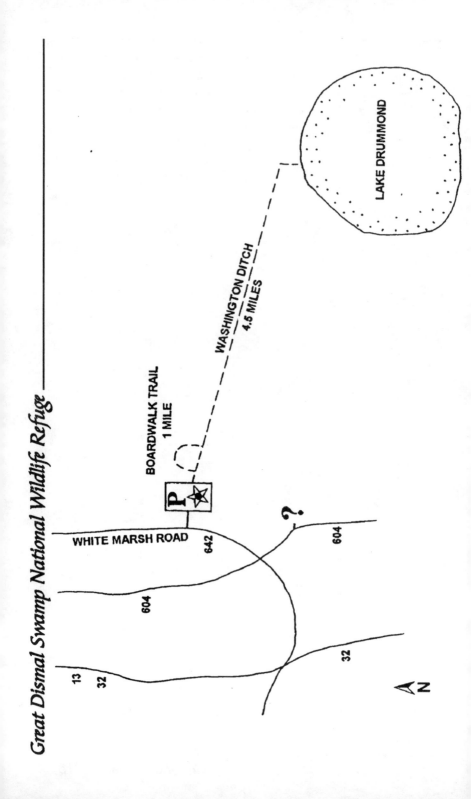

Great Dismal Swamp National Wildlife Refuge

LAKE DRUMMOND

WASHINGTON DITCH
4.5 MILES

BOARDWALK TRAIL
1 MILE

P

WHITE MARSH ROAD

642

604

604

32

13

32

N

Key

? Refuge Headquarters

P Parking

⭐ Start Here

- - - Trail

Footsteps: ─────────────────────────────

Great Dismal Swamp National Wildlife Refuge

Description

For obvious reasons, it is rare to take a nature walk through a swamp. The Washington Ditch of the Great Dismal Swamp National Wildlife Refuge offers an opportunity to experience the spectacular beauty of a swamp without getting your feet wet. The major portion of the walk is down the Washington Ditch cart path. It follows the straight line of Washington Ditch 4.5 miles to Lake Drummond. Don't skip the boardwalk to the left of the cart path at the entrance to Washington Ditch. It cuts through the swamp and provides a closer look at the mysteries of Great Dismal Swamp. Tall cypress trees with Spanish moss draped from their branches tower over you. There are two overlooks on the boardwalk. Pause at each and enjoy the sights, sounds, and scents of the swamp before the boardwalk loops back to the cart path.

The Great Dismal Swamp is one of the largest wooded wetlands in the eastern United States and offers a nature experience rarely duplicated elsewhere. It is home to over 200 species of birds. The spring migration period (April to June) is the best time to see the vast variety of birds that stop here. Many mammals inhabit the swamp, including black bear, bobcat, white-tailed deer, otter, mink, racoons, red foxes, and grey squirrels. And, for those interested, numerous varieties of reptiles and amphibians also call the Great Dismal Swamp home.

Location

Washington Ditch is located just outside Suffolk. Take I-64 East, then 664 to Rt. 58. South from Suffolk, take Rt. 13. Turn left onto Rt. 642 (White Marsh Road). Follow Rt. 642 to the parking area at Washington Ditch.

───

Parking and Facilities

There is parking available at Washington Ditch. This is an unmanned area and does not have restrooms. The Refuge Headquarters is located on Rt. 604.

Safety Tips

1. Be respectful of the wildlife. Enjoy the sights from a safe distance.

2. Insect repellent is a must in warm weather.

Background

The Great Dismal Swamp looks vastly different today than it did in the days when William Drummond first discovered Lake Drummond. William Drummond originally lived in Virginia but moved to and became the first governor of North Carolina. It is said that while hunting in 1665, the party of hunters became lost and all but Drummond died. Although weak, Drummond made it out after several days of wandering through the thick swamp. It was during this harrowing experience that he stumbled upon a lake hidden in the swamp. In addition to having Lake Drummond named after him, Drummond is also known for becoming one of Nathaniel Bacon's chief advisors when Drummond moved back to Virginia after his term as governor of North Carolina.

Changes to the swamp didn't occur until after logging and farming began. George Washington was one of the first to attempt to profit from the area. He visited the Dismal Swamp in 1763. First, he directed Nimmo Gressham to survey the swamp, then Washington and five other investors, seeing potential for use of the wetlands, formed the Dismal Swamp Land Company by investing in 40,000 acres surrounding the Washington Ditch area. He used Dismal Town on the western edge of the Washington Ditch as his headquarters for the logging and farming endeavors. In 1764, they gained permission from the Virginia Assembly to build a canal. They intended to drain and farm the swamp area west of Lake Drummond and south to North Carolina. They accomplished their goal of draining the swamp but built a ditch rather than a canal.

Ditches, of which Washington Ditch is one, were eventually built throughout the area to drain the swamp. The draining of the swamp allowed transport of harvested timber and provided easier use of the land for farming. Dirt from the ditches was used to build 140 miles of roads/cart paths. This transformation of the environment was advantageous to their efforts to use the land, but the roads also stopped the flow of water throughout the swamp and resulted in stagnant pools.

In addition to logging, the Dismal Swamp Land Company attempted to make a go of rice farming, but the endeavor never prospered. In 1768, John Washington, George's brother, became the manager of the business. By 1795, George Washington withdrew his investment in the swamp.

In 1784, the Dismal Swamp Canal Company was formed to build a canal between Virginia and North Carolina. The canal, which cuts a path down the east side of the Dismal Swamp, opened in 1805 and was built by hand. The canal is on the National Register of Historic Places and is the oldest artificial waterway in the country still in operation today. By 1820, the canal served as an important route for commercial traffic between Virginia and North Carolina. And, during the Civil War, the canal was used as a supply route for Confederate troops in Virginia.

The Jericho Ditch, which runs into Washington Ditch at the Lake Drummond end, was built in 1810. A mill was built on the ditch, but this business venture didn't prosper either. By 1812, the mill was out of business.

In 1899, William Nelson Camp bought the Land Company's swamp for $76,500. It wasn't until the 20th century that the Dismal Swamp became a refuge. Movement in this direction began in 1973. In that year, the Union Camp Company donated 49,100 acres of the swamp to the Nature Conservancy. In 1974, the Department of the Interior acquired the land, and the Dismal Swamp Act made it into a refuge.

Today, the Great Dismal Swamp National Wildlife Refuge consists of 107,000 acres of forested wetlands in Virginia and North Carolina and the 3,000 acre Lake Drummond. The Great Dismal Swamp National Wildlife Refuge is managed by the U.S. Fish and Wildlife Service. Although many of the trees were logged over the years, the area still has many beautiful bald cypress and Atlantic white-cedar trees for walkers to see.

Walks

1. *Washington Ditch Trail (4.5 miles one way to Lake Drummond):* The Washington Ditch Trail begins in the parking area. It runs parallel to Washington Ditch and offers scenic views of the swamp. Follow the trail as far as you desire and turn around to return to the parking area.

2. *Boardwalk Loop (1 mile):* The Boardwalk Loop begins to your left as you begin the Washington Ditch Trail. It winds through the swamp and exits back onto the Washington Ditch Trail.

Hog Island Wildlife Management Area

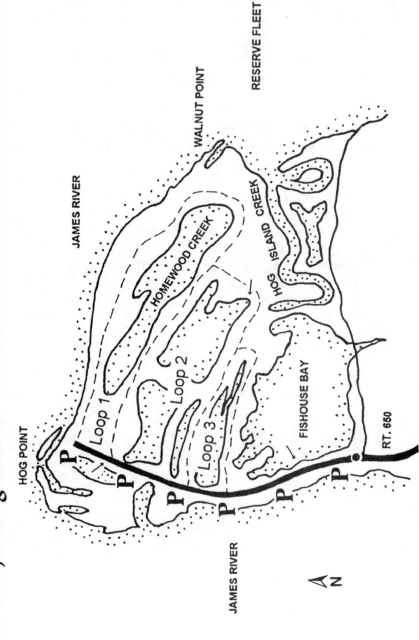

Key

Walks

Trail	Miles
Road Walk	1.8
Loop 1	3.6
Loop 2	2.7
Loop 3	1.6

- ● Entrance
- **P** Parking
- ▬ Park Road
- - - - Trail
- ← Viewing Tower

Hog Island Wildlife Management Area

Description

Hog Island Wildlife Management Area is located on a peninsula in Surry County, jutting out into the James River. The rustic paths are virtually surrounded by water and tidal marshes. Bird watchers and wildlife enthusiasts will enjoy this exceptional area. Don't forget to bring your binoculars. Except for management of the paths that take you around and through the tidal marshes and ponds, the area appears untouched by man.

There are four possible walks through the Hog Island Tract. One walk is the 1.8 mile dirt road (Rt. 650) that you can drive or walk from the wildlife management area entrance to the end of it at the James River near Hog Point. From the entrance, you'll pass through an area with views of Fishouse Bay on the right and the James River on the left. Then you'll walk through a wooded area before entering a portion of the road with breathtaking views of the ponds and Homewood Creek. There are two viewing towers on the road that allow you to survey the entire area and spot wildlife.

There are three loops to walk for a closer view of the waterfowl, wildlife, the ponds, and tidal marshes. Loop 1 is a 3.6 mile walk around Homewood Creek. On the walk, you'll see the creek and the James River on opposite sides. On the way back to the road, you'll have birdwatching opportunities as you pass the ponds and tidal marshes. Loop 2 is 2.7 miles long and passes most of the ponds. The third is 1.6 miles in length and passes ponds on one side and Fishouse Bay on the other. On all of these nature walks, you'll find an abundance of wildlife and captivating scenery.

Location

To reach Hog Island Wildlife Management Area, take Route 10 to Route 650 between the towns of Smithfield and Surry. From

Smithfield, turn right onto Route 650 and follow it to the wildlife entrance.

Parking and Facilities

There are parking areas along the road that extends from the entrance to Hog Point. Choose a parking area near the path you intend to take. This is an unmanned area: there are no restrooms and no visitor center.

Safety Tips

1. Because this area is made up of so many ponds and tidal marshes, insects can be a problem. Bring insect spray and stay on the paths.

2. Because hunting is allowed at certain times of the year, it is good to check with the Department of Game and Inland Fisheries to ensure you don't visit during one of the hunting periods.

Background

In the 17th century, English settlers let their hogs forage on this peninsula. Therefore, the area was named Hog Island. Hog Island Wildlife Management Area is 3,900 acres divided into 3 tracts.

The Hog Island Tract is at the end of the peninsula. It is a low flat area and is near sea level. A dike system is used to carefully maintain the pond system. Seasonally, the ponds are alternately drained and flooded to produce abundant food for wintering waterfowl.

Of the 2,485 acres of the Hog Island Tract, there are 200 acres of open farmland with 600 acres of pine timberland. The Department of Game and Inland Fisheries in conjunction with Duck Unlimited's M.A.R.S.H. program maintains the area and plants food for deer, dove, turkey, and quail, as well as planting wheat and milo for the waterfowl.

Two miles south of the Hog Island Tract is the Carlisle Tract. The elevation of this tract is 35 feet above sea level. Fifty acres of marshland make up part of the Carlisle Tract and the Stewart Tract next to it. There is a boat ramp at the Carlisle Tract.

Footsteps:

Bird watchers will be delighted by the varieties of migrating water-fowl, marsh birds, shore birds, and songbirds. Birds flock to the area, at times, by the thousands; especially Canada geese.

Walks

1. **Road Walk (1.8 miles):** Park in any of the nine parking areas along the road. Walk whatever distance you desire and enjoy the view of the James River and the pond and tidal marsh system.

2. **Loop 1 (3.6 miles):** Starting at the path entrance closest to the end of the dirt road, follow the path between the James River on your left and Homewood Creek on your right. After you round the corner close to Walnut Point, be sure to look out into the James River and enjoy the sight of the James River Reserve Fleet anchored off-shore. These ships are kept in good working condition at all times and can be put into action within 48 hours if needed. Walk between Homewood Creek and the pond system to return to the dirt road.

3. **Loop 2 (2.7 miles):** Starting at the viewing tower, follow the path between Homewood Creek and the pond system. Continue around this rectangular loop between the tidal marshes and ponds. Watch for animal tracks along the way and the birds in the area.

4. **Loop 3 (1.6 miles):** This loop is shorter but just as interesting as the other loops. From the road, follow the path between the ponds and return on the path between Fishouse Bay and the ponds.

Point of Interest in the Vicinity:

Bacon's Castle: Bacon's Castle is located on Route 617 off Route 650. Arthur Allen immigrated to this area in 1650 and was granted 200 acres of land. He became justice of the peace for Surry County and acquired 500 more acres next to the original 200. In 1665, he supervised the construction of Bacon's Castle. The house was built in the unusual shape of a Greek cross. Arthur Allen died only four years after the home was built.

His son, Arthur Allen, II, became the owner. He served as Speaker of the House of Burgesses and during that time Nathaniel Bacon seized the house and his forces occupied it for four months during Bacon's Rebellion. This is where the name Bacon's Castle originated. This is one of the oldest brick homes still standing in America. In 1972, the Association for the Preservation of Virginia Antiquities purchased Bacon's Castle and has maintained it since that time.

Smithfield Historic Walk

Key

? Visitor Center

P Parking

🚻 Restrooms

⭐ Start Here

‑ ‑ ‑ Walk

� Bridge

1) Old Jail
2) Old Courthouse and Clerk's Office
3) The Inn
4) Isle of Wight County Museum
5) Todd House
6) Wentworth-Barrett House
7) Wentworth-Grinnan House
8) Henning Nelms House
9) Delk House
10) King-Atkinson House
11) Eason-Whitley House
12) Pembroke Decatur Gwaltney House
13) Pembroke Decatur Gwaltney, Jr. House
14) William D. Folk House
15) Sinclair House
16) Andrew-Mackie House
17) Keitz-Mannion House
18) Watson P. Jordan House
19) Thomas Blow House
20) Wilson-Morrison House
21) Smithfield Station
22) Victorian Row
23) Pollard House
24) Hayden Hall
25) Oak Grove Academy
26) The Grove

Footsteps:
Smithfield Historic Walk

Description
When standing on the bridge over the Pagan River in the quiet town of Smithfield, known for Smithfield ham, it's easy to imagine a steamboat of the early part of this century blowing its whistle as it docks and unloads passengers returning from working or shopping in Norfolk or Newport News.

Smithfield is a friendly town filled with historic homes. The Historic District of Smithfield is a Virginia Historic Landmark and is in the National Historic Register. The town prides itself on avoiding the frenzied pace of larger cities. The walk through historic Smithfield is two miles in length and follows Smithfield's two main streets. Take this walk at a leisurely pace and enjoy the atmosphere of this small town with its Federal, Georgian and Victorian period homes, old courthouse, Isle of Wight Museum, quaint shops, and unique restaurants. You'll feel as if you've stepped back in time, especially when you notice the bronze sculptures along the walk.

Location
To reach Smithfield, take Rt. 10. When you get close to town, take Business 10 (S. Church Street) and follow it to Main Street. Turn left onto Main Street, then turn right onto Institute Street. At the next corner, turn right onto Grace Street and park on Grace Street close to the next corner (Mason Street).

Parking and Facilities
Parallel parking is available on Grace Street. Restrooms are available at the Visitor Center at 130 Main Street. There are numerous shops and restaurants to enjoy in Smithfield.

Background
The Warascoyak (Warrosquyoake) Indians were the original inhab-

itants of the area now known as Smithfield in Isle of Wight County. The town of Smithfield was slow to develop and this may be the reason it has remained a quiet, quaint river town to this day.

Smithfield is named for Arthur Smith, who, in 1637, patented 1450 acres along the Pagan River in Isle of Wight. It wasn't until 1750 that Arthur Smith IV had the land surveyed into four streets and seventy-two lots.

Smithfield started and thrived as a river town. It was used as a port for tobacco, cured ham, bacon and corn. Other products included peanuts, lumber and produce. The town activity centered around the river. The steamboat whistle awakened the inhabitants of Smithfield and called them to their jobs or school. Again, in the evenings, the steamboat whistle pulled the community together to greet those returning from the day in Norfolk or Newport News. Each evening, many of the citizens would respond to the whistle and meet the boat.

Because Smithfield became the center of commerce for the area, the county seat was moved from Glebe Farm to Smithfield in 1752. It served as the county seat for approximately 50 years. In 1779, Captain Mallory Todd established the first curing and shipping business. The first shipment of Smithfield ham was made in that same year. The other industry in the early days was the peanut cleaning and packing company. Established by Pembroke Decatur Gwaltney and Augustus Bunkley, the company put out 45 million pounds of peanuts per year by 1905.

The businesses thrived until 1921 when the peanut factory caught fire. Without sufficient firefighting equipment, the fire spread to the meat factories, and the town was filled with the smell of burning peanuts and smoldering lard. Around this same period, Suffolk was also establishing a peanut industry. After the fire, Suffolk took over the peanut industry, but the cured meat industry stayed in Smithfield. To this day, the meat industry is the heart of Smithfield's economy.

Walk
Begin the walk on Grace Street. Turn right onto Mason Street,

Footsteps:

followed by a left turn onto Main Street. At the light, turn right onto S. Church Street and continue to the middle of the bridge over the Pagan River. Turn around and walk back up S. Church Street to Main Street. Turn left onto Main Street. Follow Main Street to Drummonds Lane. At Drummonds Lane cross to the other side of Main Street. Turn right onto Cary Street then right onto Grace Street and return to where you parked.

Points of Interest

1. *Old Jail (106 N. Mason St.):* This building was built in 1799 by Isaac Lever, just one year before the courthouse and jail were moved. It has been a private residence since the jail was moved in 1800.

2. *Old Courthouse and Clerk's Office (Visitor Center) (130 Main St.):* The Old Courthouse was originally built in 1750 and served as the courthouse for the area for 50 years. The rounded main courtroom was designed after the old capitol in Williamsburg. After this building ceased being used as the courthouse, the building was used as a private dwelling. In 1959, the Association for the Preservation of Virginia Antiquities restored it. Today, it is used as a Visitor's Center and it houses the Chamber of Commerce.

3. *The Inn (Smithfield Inn and Tavern) (112 Main St.):* In 1752, this building was built by Henry Woodley. William Rand operated a tavern here, starting in 1759. In 1854, the Christ Episcopal Church bought it and used it as the rectory.

4. *Isle of Wight County Museum (103 Main St.):* Today this building houses local historical artifacts and a gift shop. Originally, it was built to house the Bank of Smithfield.

5. *Todd House (22 Main St.):* This was the home of Captain Mallory Todd who began the meat curing business in Smithfield. He made the first shipment of Smithfield ham in 1779. The left wing was built around 1753 by Nicholas Parker. Thomas House is next door to Todd House on the corner of Main St. and S. Church St. It was built in 1889 for Richard S. Thomas. It was nicknamed "Mansion on Main" because it was the larg-

est home in Smithfield. This beautiful Victorian house has been restored as a bed and breakfast.

6. *Wentworth-Barrett House (117 S. Church St.):* Built in 1752. Captain Samuel Wentworth, captain of the ship, Sallie, lived in this house. It was one of the first buildings in Smithfield. Fred Barrett, II restored it in the 1950's.

7. *Wentworth-Grinnan House (123 S. Church St.):* Built in 1780.

8. *Henning Nelms House (205 S. Church St.):* Built in 1882. One of Smithfield's mayors lived in this house.

9. *Delk House (212 S. Church St.):* This house was built in 1877. Captain O.G. Delk served in Kemper's Brigade during the Civil War and was one of Smithfield's captains of the steamboat, Hampton Roads. Each morning, he loaded passengers and fresh produce and headed down river.

10. *King-Atkinson House (213 S. Church St.):* Built in 1798. This house was occupied at one time by Thomas King who served in the Revolutionary War. It was occupied later by Captain Joseph Atkinson. He served in the War of 1812.

11. *Eason-Whitley House (220 S. Church St.):* Built between 1752 and 1756. This house stands on one of the first lots sold after Arthur Smith, IV had the area surveyed and divided into 72 lots. James Eason lived here starting in 1756. The Whitley family has owned it since 1913.

12. *Pembroke Decatur Gwaltney House (226 S. Church St.):* Pembroke Decatur Gwaltney founded the peanut business in Smithfield and the meat curing and packing company. This house was built in 1876 and is still owned by the Gwaltney family.

13. *Pembroke Decatur Gwaltney, Jr. House (304 S. Church St.):* Built in 1901.

14. **William D. Folk House (309 S. Church St.):** Built in 1876. This house has been the home of three of Smithfield's mayors: William D. Folk, 1884 - 1893; Howard Gwaltney, 1950 - 1961; and Florine H. Moore, elected in 1986.

15. ***Sinclair House (335 S. Church St.):** This house was occupied by Captain John Sinclair from 1778 - 1796. He brought supplies for the colonies during the Revolutionary War. After the war, it is thought that he became a pirate.

16. ***Andrew-Mackie House (338 S. Church St.):** Built in 1796. This house has a beautiful formal garden area designed in the colonial style.

17. **Keitz-Mannion House (344 S. Church St.):** Built in 1876. The back of the house became the front when it was moved from across the street. It was built as the Methodist parsonage.

18. **Watson P. Jordan House (351 S. Church St.):** Built around 1820. This was the home of Archibald Atkinson. He served in the U.S. Congress in the mid-1800's.

19. **Thomas Blow House (352 S. Church St.):** Built around 1800. This is a Federal style home. It was built for Mrs. Francis Marshall Boykin, who was the widow of General Boykin. General Boykin served during the Revolutionary War. Fort Boykin on the James River was named after him.

20. ***Wilson-Morrison House (365 S. Church St.):** Built in 1775.

21. **Smithfield Station:** This waterfront inn and restaurant is a perfect spot to enjoy the river.

22. **Victorian Row (336 - 346 Main St.):** Burton W. Heam built these five Victorian-style houses around 1901.

23. ***Pollard House (108 Cary St.):** Built in 1750. This house used to be on Main Street but was moved onto Cary Street around 1800.

24. *Hayden Hall (222 Grace St.):* This brick residence was built in 1812 for Mrs. Martha Hall. In 1825, Mrs. Julia Hayden moved to Smithfield. She is mainly credited with the development of the educational system of Smithfield. She used this building briefly in 1836 for an academy for young girls before it moved to the Oak Grove Academy building. It was called the Smithfield Female Institute.

25. *Oak Grove Academy (204 Grace St.):* In 1836, the Oak Grove Academy for Young Ladies was built. It housed the Smithfield Female Institute. Mrs. Julia Hayden's successor, Mrs. Sallie Anne Eley, made it so successful that it was opened to young men as well and was renamed, the Smithfield Male and Female Institute.

26. **The Grove (220 Grace St.):* Built between 1780 and 1790. It was once used as a boarding house.

*18th century structures

Point of Interest in the Vicinity

St. Luke's Church: Two miles south of Smithfield on Rt. 10, this beautiful church is a National Shrine. It is open February 1 to December 31, Tuesday through Sunday from 10:00am until 4:00pm. It is closed on major holidays. As St. Luke's Church is a shrine, it is not a working church, but it is used for special events, such as weddings and concerts during the year. It is the oldest church of English foundation in America and the only Gothic church building in the United States. It dates back to 1632 and is adorned with beautiful stained glass windows, a 17th century communion table, and silver baptismal basin.

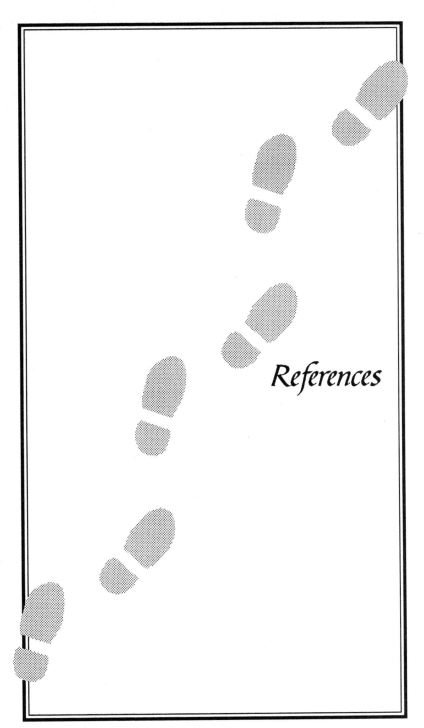

References

Adkins, Leonard M. *Seashore State Park: A Walking Guide.* Centreville, Maryland: Tidewater Publishers, 1990

Arthur, Colonel Robert and Weinert, Richard P., Jr. *Defender of the Chesapeake: The Story of Fort Monroe.* Shippensburg, Pennsylvania: White Mane Publishing Co, Inc., 1989

Bailey, Bill *Virginia State Parks.* Saginaw, Michigan: Glovebox Guidebooks of America, 1996

Barbour, Philip L. *The Jamestown Voyages Under the First Charter - Volume 1.* London: Cambridge University Press, 1969

Billings, Warren M. *Jamestown and the Founding of the Nation.* Gettysburg, Pennsylvania: Thomas Publications

Bruno, Michael H. and McPeters, Annette *The Insider's Guide to Williamsburg, Jamestown, Yorktown.* Manteo, North Carolina: Insiders' Guides, Inc., 1993

Carroll, Steven R. And Miller, Mark *Wilderness Virgjnia, A Guide to Hiking Virginia's National Forest Wilderness Areas.* Lexington, Virginia: Old Forge Productions, 1995

Colonial Williamsburg Official Guidebook and Map. Williamsburg, Virginia, 1972

Compiled by Workers of the Writer's Program of the Work Projects Administration in the State of Virginia *Virginia: A Guide to the Old Dominion.* New York: Oxford University Press, 1940. Richmond: Virginia State Library and Archives, 1992

Dabney, Virginius *Virginia - The New Dominion.* Charlottesville: University of Virginia Press, 1971

De Hart, Allen *The Trails of Virginia, Hiking the Old Dominion.* Chapel Hill, North Carolina: The University of North Carolina Press, 1995

Dixon, Suzy Adams and Hartman, Sally Kirby *The Insider's Guide to Virginia Beach/Norfolk.* Manteo, North Carolina: The Insiders' Guides, Inc., 1993

Farrar, Emmie Ferguson *Old Virginia Houses Along the James.* New York: Bonanza Book, 1957

Farrar, Emmie Ferguson and Hines, Emilee *Old Virginia Houses - Harbors.* Charlotte, North Carolina: Delmar Publishing, 1984

Fridell, Guy *Hello, Hampton Roads.* The Future of Hampton Roads, Inc., 1987

Gloucester County and Gloucester Historical Committee *Gloucester County, Virginia - Landmarks.* Gloucester, Va.: Prestige Press, Inc., 1983

Hartman, Sally Kirby and Ingersol, Ridgely *The Insider's Guide to Virginia's Chesapeake Bay.* Manteo, North Carolina: Insiders' Guides, Inc., 1996

Hume, Ivor Noel *Here Lies Virginia.* New York: Alfred A. Knopf, 1963

Johnson, Randy *Hiking Virginia.* Helena, Montana: Falcon Press Publishing Co., Inc., 1992

Lancaster, Robert A., Jr. *Historic Virginia Homes and Churches* Philadelphia and London: J.P. Lippincott Company, 1915

Mariner, Kirk *Once Upon An Island - The History of Chincoteague.* New Church, Virginia: Minona Publications, 1996

Miller, Everett L. And Cohen, Jay S. *The American Garden Guidebook.* New York: M. Evans and Co., Inc., 1987

Mulligan, Tim *Virginia: A History and Guide.* New York: Random House, 1986

Ockershausen Smith, Jane *One Day Trips Through History.* McLean, Virginia: EPM Publications, Inc., 1982

Ockershausen Smith, Jane *The Virginia One Day Trip Book.* McLean, Virginia: EPM Publications, Inc., 1986

Official Guide to Colonial Williamsburg Williamsburg, Virginia: Colonial Williamsburg Foundation, 1985

O'Neal, William B. *Architecture in Virginia* New York: Walker and Company, Inc., 1968

Parramore, Thomas C. with Stewart, Peter C. And Bogger, Tommy L. *Norfolk: The First Four Centuries.* Chalottesville and London: University Press of Virginia, 1995

Peters, John O., Peters, Margaret T. *Virginia's Historic Courthouses.* Charlottesville and London: University Press of Virginia, 1995

Rawlings, James Scott *Virginia's Colonial Churches: An Architectural Guide* Richmond: Garrett and Massie, 1963

Roundtree, Helen C. *The Powhatan Indians of Virginia* Norman and London: University of Oklahoma Press, 1989

Rouse, Parke, Jr. *Tidewater Virginia In Color* New York: Hastings House Publishers, 1988

Salmon, John S. *A Guidebook to Virginia's Historical Markers.* Charlottesville and London: University Press of Virginia, 1994

Simpson, Bland *The Great Dismal* Chapel Hill: University of North Carolina Press, 1990

Trudell, Clyde F. *Colonail Yorktown.* Gettysburg, Pennsylvania: Thomas Publications, 1971

Virginia Landmarks Register. Charlottesville, Virginia: University Press of Virginia, 1986

Walker, Carroll *Norfolk: A Tricentennial Pictorial History.* Norfolk, Virginia: The Donning Company/Publishers, 1981

Footsteps: _____

Wenger, Mark R. *Carter's Grove - A Story of a Virginia Plantation.* Williamsburg, Virginia: The Colonial Williamsburg Foundation, 1994

Winegar, Deane and Winegar, Garvey   *Natural Wonders of Virginia.* Castine Maine: Country Road Press, 1994

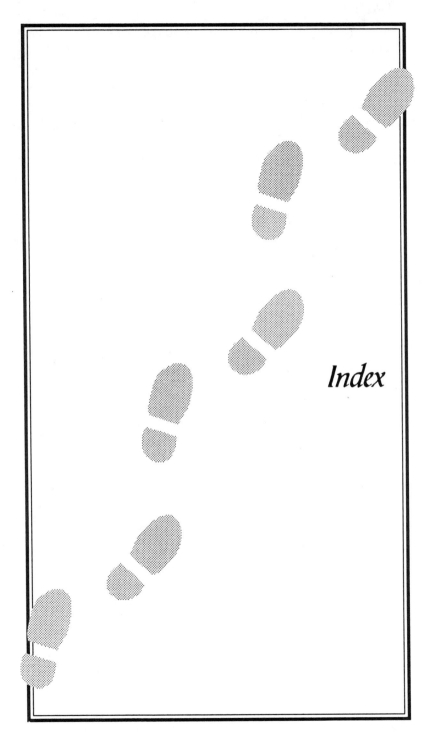

Index

Footsteps: ————————————————————————

Footsteps:

ORDER FORM

Please send _____ copies of *Footsteps: Unfor-gettable Walks in Southeastern Virginina*
@ $12.95 per copy to:

Name: _____

Address: _____

Apt. No.: _____

City: _____

State: _____

Zip Code: _____

Quantity _____ x $12.95   Amount: _____

4.5 % Sales Tax in Va.   *Shipping and handling

*Shipping and handling: Add $3.00 for the first
book, 75 cents for each additional book.

                                    Total: _____

Make check payable to Footsteps, Inc. and mail
to:

Footsteps, Inc.
P.O. Box 2302
Chesapeake, Virginia 23327-2302

ORDER FORM

Please send _____ copies of _Footsteps: Unforgettable Walks in Southeastern Virginina_ @ $12.95 per copy to:

Name: _____
Address: _____
Apt. No.: _____
City: _____
State: _____
Zip Code: _____

Quantity_____ x $12.95   Amount:_____

4.5 % Sales Tax in Va.   *Shipping and handling

*Shipping and handling: Add $3.00 for the first book, 75 cents for each additional book.

Total: _____

Make check payable to Footsteps, Inc. and mail to:

Footsteps, Inc.
P.O. Box 2302
Chesapeake, Virginia 23327-2302